Praise for *How to Butter Toast*

'A total joy. Part Dr Seuss, part Ogden Nash, part Julia Child, 100% inspired and inspiring.' Samin Nosrat

'In just a couple of hours reading it, I feel I've learned more than from reading dozens of recipes. It's something to dip into and return to with delight. A lovely kitchen companion.' Bee Wilson

'Fun and wise, Tara manages to capture the kinds of the things we cogitate about – sometimes without even knowing! – and provides reassuring answers to those confusing everyday conundrums. A collection for when you are weary of recipes and cooking, but not of life itself!' Helen Goh

'I can't think of many food authorities who can string together words which are as poignant and profound as they are entertaining and ear-pleasing.' Yotam Ottolenghi

'Wigley's book has the makings of a modern classic. Imagine the literary love child that might have resulted had Dr Seuss eloped with Elizabeth David.' *Wall Street Journal*

'Charming' Nigella Lawson

Praise for *How the Cookie Crumbles*

'Some of the greatest kitchen conundrums – solved, clarified, demystified. With her signature rhythm and rhymes, Tara has found a one-off way of shedding light on the niggling questions food lovers love to obsess over. And even if you *don't* tend to lose too much sleep over the difference between a pumpkin and squash, say, or between an ice cream and a gelato, you will surely be tickled. As ever with Tara, this is informative and entertaining!' Yotam Ottolenghi

Pavilion
An imprint of HarperCollins*Publishers*
Ltd
1 London Bridge Street
London SE1 9GF

www.harpercollins.co.uk

HarperCollins*Publishers*
Macken House
39/40 Mayor Street Upper,
Dublin 1
D01 C9W8
Ireland

10 9 8 7 6 5 4 3 2 1

First published in Great Britain by
Pavilion
An imprint of HarperCollins*Publishers*
2025

ISBN 978-0-00-855473-6

Publishing Director: Laura Russell
Commissioning Editor: Lucy Smith
Editorial Assistant: Daisy Gudmunsen
Design Manager: Alice Kennedy-Owen
Illustrator: Alec Doherty
Artworker: Hannah Naughton
Proofreader: Angela Koo
Production Controller: Grace O'Byrne

Printed and bound by RR Donnelley
in China

WHEN USING KITCHEN
APPLIANCES PLEASE ALWAYS
FOLLOW THE MANUFACTURER'S
INSTRUCTIONS

tara wigley

how the
cookie
crumbles

PAVILION

Magic one, four, two ratio,
Sugar, spirits and lime…
The drinks start to flow
Thanks to one little rhyme!

You'll be relieved to know this will be my only foray into verse
in this foreword, or indeed elsewhere, because, unlike Tara,
I have neither rhythm nor beauty in my soul. I love poetry,
but these days, I find I have more time for the down-to-earth,
useful kind than the lofty epics of my student days, when I
had nothing better to do than wander lonely as a cloud in
someone else's imagination. There's a reason why children's
counting rhymes like 'one, two, buckle my shoe' have hung
on since the days of George III, or why we all still mentally
whisper 'thirty days hath September' when trying to work out
when we're likely to get paid; rhythms and rhymes have a way
of lodging in our memories in a way that dry old prose never
can… which is why I'm such a big fan of this book.

Along with *How to Butter Toast*, Tara's first foray into the
world of culinary poetry, it feels like a collection that will
earn its place on kitchen shelves long after most of its glossy
contemporaries have been replaced by newer models –
because what we first read with delight and, I'm afraid, in the
case of '*Whatever drink you choose, enjoy, but think to stop at
one/Though cocktails can make out that all they are is liquid
fun/they can be strong (and guarantee you will look like a fool/
when, after drinking, three or four, you do fall off that stool)*',
bashful recognition has a funny way of coming in handy
further down the line.

Though almost anyone can follow someone else's recipe, I firmly believe that to be a good cook, by which I mean an adaptable, practical cook who can make a decent meal out of almost anything, you first need to absorb a few basic laws and rules to be pulled out of your hat as required – like when to use a new potato versus an… old one, for example. But though I thought I already knew everything about that particular subject, being intimately familiar with the (personally much-missed) British Potato Council table of dry matter by variety, I learnt several things from this chapter – including exactly *why* starchy potatoes are the superior choice for chips, which I'd never stopped to ponder before. Similarly, I now have a succinct answer to the question 'What's the difference between pasta and noodles', and a fighting chance of remembering how to convert Fahrenheit to Celsius… and thanks to a dash of fun, all this education slipped down as easily as an ice-cold daiquiri (four parts light rum, two parts lime, one part sugar syrup).

In fact, this book is the perfect illustration of the old saying 'You catch more flies with honey than vinegar', which is fairly poetic in itself, now I come to think of it. I wonder what Tara has to say about honey…

Felicity Cloake

Introduction

These rhymes compare two things that often tend to
   get conflated
and, in doing so, confusion reigns as meaning is debated.

So, it's only when we stop and really question what we mean
that we see what makes a sorbet, not gelato (or ice cream).

That a muffin, versus cupcake, is quite separate from the start;
that a quiche is not a pie and that a pie is not a tart.

And that quiche is not tortilla, and tortilla's not frittata,
and an ocean is what makes distinct an 'entree' from a 'starter'

And a chef is not the same as cook: to merge the two is wrong,
and a macaroon is not to be confused with macaron.

Setting ovens to conventional is not the same as fan,
and a jelly is its own thing: it is jelly, not a jam.

Muesli, bircher or granola: all as one when in a bowl,
but they all have their distinct traits (like a bun or bap or roll).

And a noting of the gap is so important, for it traces
what the links are when it comes to food and history,
    people, places.

For it's always more than just a 'bap' or 'cob' or 'roll' or 'bun';
it's these names that tell us who we are and from where we
    have come.

So sit down and settle in, with tea (or any hot infusion),
as we sort out all the works and quirks of culinary confusion.

Just make sure – for those with tea in hand – it's biscuits
    in the tin;
cookies crumble – tea disaster! Those confused?
    Then let's begin…

what's the difference between

granola,

muesli

and

bircher?

Oats and nuts, some fruit and seeds: all three might have all four,
but bircher (which *is* muesli) is untoasted – it is raw.
The thing that makes it *bircher* (which translates as 'little mush')
is that it needs some prep and soaking: it's not one to rush.

This little bowl of mush became a thing when one Swiss man
saw, in raw food, the benefits – he was a massive fan.
His name was Bircher-Benner, he had recently been sick,
then found that fruit and veg, uncooked, made him get
    better quick.

He had his realization when out hiking with his wife
and saw the role that food could play in healthy shepherd life.
He set about to recreate the Alpine hiking taste.
It was the 1890s; it was new to be veg-based.

A bowl of oats and grated apple, milk (condensed and sweet)
made up the mix, with lemon juice, that Benner said to eat.
It needed to be soaked a while to be the real deal,
and eaten – just a little – at the start of every meal.

Nuts were also added as a welcome, clean addition:
all part of Benner's strong belief in raw food as nutrition.
He opened up a spa to help his Zurich patients see
the benefits of what he called his 'order therapy'.

Across the seas, around this time, in New York, USA,
a similar discovery had been set underway.
There was a Dr Jackson based in Dansville, New York State,
who made a mix of crumbled Graham flour, which he baked.

He called it 'Jackson's granula', he linked it to good health.
He served it in his spa to those infirm (but blessed with wealth).
Jackson was, like Benner, somewhat evangelical
about the fact that healthy food could make a person well.

The spa, it's said – a few months on – then welcomed in a guest
who seemed, perhaps, a little *too* inspired by his rest.
His name was Dr John Harvey (he had not yet gained fame);
'Kellogg' was this patient's soon-to-be-well-known surname.

Once he left the spa, John (with his other Kellogg brother)
came up with 'their' own granula (which called to mind another)
Jackson was so angry that he set about and sued
these brothers who were passing off as *theirs* his own
  health food.

The Kelloggs had to change the name to clear up any doubt.
They came up with 'granola', which they quickly then rolled out.
Granola at this time, though, was still seen as 'food as cure';
Kellogg was a healthy man – the life he lived was pure.

It wasn't till the sixties that granola went mainstream.
Taken up by hippies with their back-to-nature dream.
Peace and love and cereal: it was the hippy way –
oats and milk (and flower power), seeing in each day.

Over time, additions came, with honey and dried fruit.
After 1970, most claims to health were moot.
The sweeter that it got, the more it played a major role
in being something poured into the morning breakfast bowl.

The more that children turned to it, the sweeter it became.
The hippy-healthy connotations soon began to wane.
Maple syrup, chocolate chips or turned into a bar:
all *quite* a way from Jackson's vision, eaten in his spa.

Granola's now a morning treat, granola can be lunch.
Granola is a snack that always has a toasted crunch.
Muesli, on the other hand, health-wise is still okay:
there are, indeed, worse ways to set you up for every day.

If you *really* want to make the claim for 'food as health',
the only option, really, is to make it up yourself.
Oats and nuts and fruit and seeds – the combination's loose –
soaked, or eaten as it is with milk or apple juice.

Add whatever fruit's in season, maybe add some spice.
Cinnamon and nutmeg are both really very nice.
See what's in the cupboard: it's okay to have a forage,
but if the mix is too oat-based – watch out, you have
    made porridge!

what's the difference between

Marmite

and Bovril?

They are both pastes, which look, to some, a little bit like tar:
they're dark and thick and spread on toast; they have a
   bulbous jar.
But though they look the same, they represent two
   different sides:
they're *much* more than a breakfast choice; they're one of
   life's divides.

'Left' or 'right'? Forget, for now, the politics you choose:
it's second to the spread you have and love to eat and use.
An overview of history, of how each are made and taste
is useful to inform our knowledge of each separate paste.

Bovril was the prototype: the first to come along –
it came onto the market thanks to one Napoleon.
His nineteenth-century army was so hungry and in need
of food that would sustain the troops, keep well, and also feed.

The call put out was answered by a Scottish businessman;
John Lawson Johnston found a way to put beef in a can.
A reason why his 'fluid beef' went on to really sell,
was that it had a long shelf life and travelled really well.

But though John Johnston did, indeed, so very well from war,
his market was decreasing after 1884.
War was, he knew, no long-term plan; in order to stay great
he needed other customers, so had to relocate.

Attention turned from soldiers, then, to home-creating wives,
who built it into what they ate as part of daily lives.
It soon was used to boost the flavour of each soup and stew
or simply mixed with boiling water for a hearty brew.

So that was Bovril, years went on and soon the century turned,
it was now that a scientist from Germany soon learned
that what is left – the yeast extract – once beer is made
   and brewed,
can also be converted into something sold as food.

Justus Liebig was his name, he thought it simply great
to make a veggie, yeasty, paste-like dark-brown concentrate.
A few more things – some salt and spices – in these also went
to what was known as 'Marmite', made in Burton-upon-Trent.

As well as this, the ration packs that went to World War One
included jars of Marmite so that helped to get 'job done'.
For it was also at this time that vitamins were known
to help the health of those at war, and also those at home.

Diseases could be curbed by taking B12, 1 and 2.
Step forward, Marmite, here we go – this is the job for you!
Once Marmite was established as a tasty, easy source
of such a range of vitamins it was embraced, of course.

As years went by, the sales of both the brown spreads were
   quite strong,
till some considered Bovril to be somehow sort of, *wrong*.
When challenged by the die-hard fans who asked 'what',
   'why' and 'how?'
the doubters said, 'Well, think of it: it's made from liquid cow.'

'For all that cows are great, and all, and make for tasty meat,
they're something we prefer to cook and cut and chew and eat.
It's beer – not cow – we want to pour: it's beer we want to drink.
So Marmite, which is veggie, just makes more sense, we all think.'

But Marmite, too, was something which could really polarize,
so it was very smart and bold for those who thought it wise
to have a slogan that embraced the choice to 'LOVE!' or 'HATE!':
to make a statement out of what we put upon our plate.

The slogan really struck a nerve: it proved to be so strong,
that something being 'Marmite' is now in our lexicon.
The two spreads can now share an aisle but stand as
   separate troops,
two coloured-coded (red and yellow) beefy, yeasty groups.

Why is Bovril called Bovril? And Marmite called Marmite?

It is a portmanteau, the 'Bo' is taken from 'bo-vine',
the '-vril' was taken from a book, well known around this time.
It was invented in *The Coming Race*: this was the book:
a science-fiction novel where the 'Vril-ya' people took
some kind of strong, electrical and energizing force
(a connotation that sat well with Bovril's brand, of course).

Staffordshire was not the place that 'Marmite's' name began:
this was, instead, from France where *marmite* was a
   cooking pan
in which a stock or soup is made and cooks low on a simmer,
so conjuring up thoughts and smells of what might be
   for dinner.
The marmite pan was metal and it had the bulbous shape
that Marmite – as a spread – once in its jar would also take.

what's the difference between

a cupcake

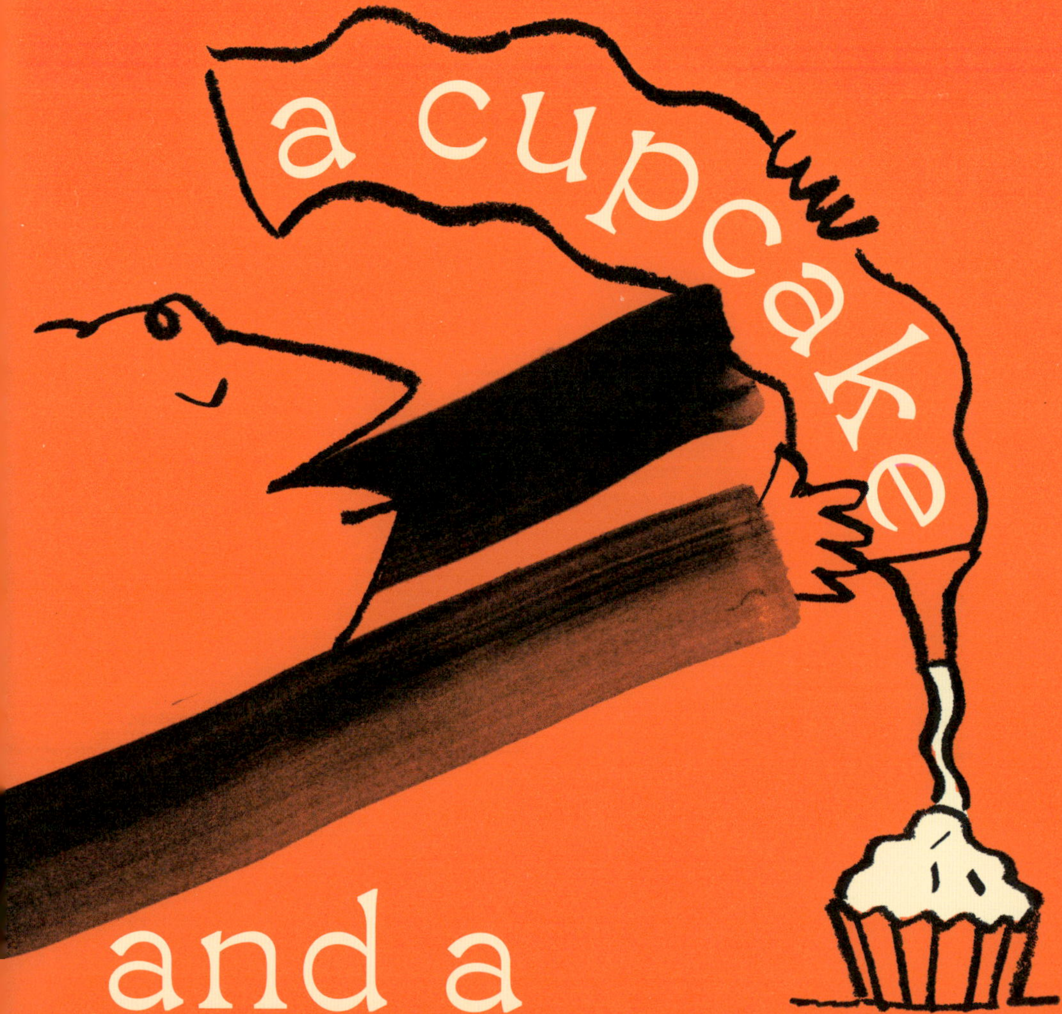

and a

muffin?

A muffin and a cupcake are both single-serving bakes.
So, what is it that separates these little hand-held cakes?
Is a muffin not a cupcake that has failed to be iced?
And a cupcake just a fairy cake which is, then, overpriced?!

Dealing first with icing, since we've said already that
cupcakes always have it, as their surface is quite flat.
Being flat and level means that they are primed to fit,
and support, the piped-up frosting (which can then securely sit).

Frosting, on a muffin, would not work or be that wise
for the cake itself has domed up: formed an arch, a curve, a rise.
It can also mushroom out and have a rim that is quite wide
so the extras that are wanted, get securely baked *inside*.

If a muffin tends to look quite plain (here 'rustic' is the word),
cupcakes can be so adorned, they look, at times, absurd.
There are, though, certain factors (not just simply how they look)
which show them as distinct: how they are made and mixed
   and cook.

The basic batter mix is pretty similar, for sure:
flour, butter, sugar, eggs (though cupcakes will have more:
sugar, butter – both increased – which, as a rule of thumb
will lead, when baked, to something sweet that has a moist,
    fine crumb).

Muffins also tend to have some yoghurt in the batter
(or buttermilk works just as well: the acid is what matters).
The acid works in tandem with the raising agent there,
which then helps the batter rise up as it fills with holes of air.

The *way* these things are mixed up is a factor, too, at play.
For these are two different batters, which are made a
    different way.
'Creaming' is the practice that all cupcakes tend to preach.
It's the basic 'beat the butter with the sugar' all cakes teach.

Once it's light and fluffy and the eggs are beaten in,
it's the flour that is added next before it's in the tin.
The batter is quite loose: for cupcakes this is deemed just right
as the cake that it will make will then be fluffy, cloudy, light.

Muffins, on the other hand, are denser as a rule.
Their batter does not need a high-speed fancy mixing tool.
A wooden spoon is perfect (and a little elbow power),
just to mix the wet ingredients into the bowl of flour.

Because it is not whisked (and is just stirred by hand instead),
the texture of the muffin batter is a bit like bread.
The bread-like muffin batter means that these can either be
sweet (with fruit or chocolate chips) or else they work
　　when savoury.

Courgette nicely grated (plus some feta) is one way
that a muffin can be eaten at the start of every day.
Cupcakes, on the other hand, are seen more as a treat
as their icing means that they are never less than *very* sweet.

Muffins are an all-day thing, while cupcakes are dessert
(though every now and then a breakfast cupcake will not hurt).
The only thing that hurts (for those who bake and charge
　　a bomb)
is the thinking that they're basically the same: *that is just wrong*!

what's the difference between

jam

and

jelly?

Jam and jelly are preserves we like to make and eat,
both of which need fruit and sugar, and some form of heat.
The thing that takes them down their separate jam or jelly route
is how much, once they're made, they still consist of actual fruit.

For jam is made from real fruit, chopped up (or first pureed),
while jelly starts with fruit juice, from which it's cooked and
    then made.
While jam can range in texture from the chunky to the smooth,
for jelly, only clarity's the look that is approved.

Jelly's made by cooking down the whole fruit: skin and flesh,
which is then slowly passed on through a soft, clean, fabric mesh.
The juice is then what's saved to use, the pulp can disappear,
for jelly wants no seeds or chunks; it only prizes clear.

Either way, they both need lots of sugar and they get
some pectin, which is then what helps the jam (or jelly) set.
Pectin is the natural gel that's always found within
the pith and core and pips of fruit (and also in its skin).

Some fruit is low on pectin so, when cooked, stays far too loose,
unless it's helped by pectin-high fruit, and some lemon juice.
Apples are a classic pairing, helping things along:
working with the juice, they make the pectin networks strong.

Gooseberries, on the other hand, would naturally set well.
Because they're quite acidic, they can form the fruity gel.
If jam, once cooked, should be a soft and spreadable firm paste,
jelly's firmness is 'its thing', as crucial as the taste.

Or compote, curd, marmalade and chutney?

It's not just jam and jelly from which fruit and sugar's made.
There's compote and there's curd and there is bitter
   marmalade.
The latter's made from oranges (or lemons, also limes):
it has – as well as fruit and pulp – the tangy citrus rinds.

The rind is either thick-cut or it can be shredded thin
but, if it's marmalade, the rind will always be left in.
Because of all the pectin that the rind will hence contain,
what's made is always firm (and often from Seville, in Spain).

Compote, though it's made from fruit and sugar, is best viewed
as a distant cousin, really – fruit just slowly stewed.
No other agent's added to help make it firmly set,
so the shelf life on the jar is all you're ever going to get.

Any fruit will work here, juicy berries are quite fun.
Or cherries – their deep colour! – with some apples, pear
   or plum.
There might be added sugar, and some spices will not hurt,
before it's served with cream or custard as a quick dessert.

Chutney is another jam to mention – it deserves
a place when we are thinking of the world of fruit preserves.
The name includes a range of condiments and fiery dips,
but there's no extra pectin and no fruity peel or pips.

Instead, these chunks of fruit are cooked with vinegar
    and spice.
It's often served in India, with curry and some rice.
Mostarda is quite similar, in Italy it pleases
those in the North, who serve it with boiled meat and
    also cheeses.

But all this talk of meat and cheese and curries in our belly
has taken us a little way from simple jam and jelly.
In summary, there are a few jam facts to spread and learn:
that jelly's clear, while jam is not, and jelly's always firm.

Jam goes inside a doughnut, it is layered in a cake.
It's always on a scone, where there are further things at stake.
Depending on allegiance – Cornwall, Devon: pick a team
to establish which goes first: is it the jam or clotted cream?

Jelly-one, jelly-two, jelly-three, jelly-o

Jelly, as a term, is used in three ways – all are 'right'.
First, jelly sweets (think jelly babies and Turkish delight).
A gelling agent's needed so that things don't then unfold,
some starch or gelatin to make the setting fruit juice hold.

Gelatin (or there are veggie options if one wishes)
plays a role in option two: the jellied pudding dishes.
These jellies that set in a mould, then sit there looking great,
with their little wibble-wobble, on a serving plate.

The third group is the one jarred up (as if it were a jam):
things like quince or crab apple that work so well with ham.
This jelly can be savoury as much as it is sweet.
Just think of green mint jelly, which works very well with meat.

(There is, of course, a fourth group in the big US of A,
where 'jelly' is the word for 'jam' so that is what you say.
If you want some 'jelly' for dessert, the thing to know,
is that the 'y' gets subbed out: it's converted to Jell-O).

Frittatas and tortillas: are they just a separate name
for two types of thick, flat omelette, which are otherwise
　　the same?
We know they both have things inside that eggs, once cooked,
　　will bind,
but, slicing up the two, what point of difference do we find?

Tortillas are the Spanish ones: they're major tapas players.
Potatoes, which have been sliced thin, create the rustic layers.
A waxy kind works best; it means the slices hold their shape
(the floury ones would break down so a mush is what
　　you'd make).

The spuds need lots of olive oil and cook best long and slow
with onions, sliced thin as well – though purists here say 'no!'
They think a true *tortilla de patatas* is just that:
eggs (whisked up), potatoes (sliced) and cooked in ample fat.

Those who go for onions, though, rightly wonder why
you'd skip them out; they're sweet and also stop things
　　getting dry.
They bring a welcome moisture which, with eggs,
　　is rarely wrong
and with tortilla *crucial*: it dries out if cooked too long.

The way the dish is cooked is where the difference is most great.
Tortillas get inverted, once half-set, onto a plate.
They're then slid back into the pan and cook on 'upside down':
it means both sides are neat and smooth and neither one
   too brown.

Frittatas, on the other hand, though starting on the hob,
will move below the oven grill to finish off the job.
The top will therefore colour and things sticking out will 'catch',
which means the base and top (unlike tortilla) will not match.

But while tortillas pride themselves on both sides being smooth,
Italians don't mind at all and feel no need to prove.
They see their own frittatas as a rustic dish – not chic –
'Our version of an omelette: just without the French mystique'.

If tortillas have potatoes and inversions as their tricks,
frittatas often find themselves with dairy in their mix.
It can be milk, or cream, or cheese, but dairy is a must.
It's this that makes some think of it as 'quiche without the crust'.

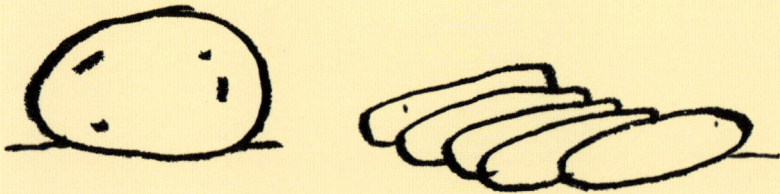

For, as with quiche, the dairy makes the texture that of custard.
Once cooked, 'the wobble' is the thing that makes it cut
    the mustard.
The fillings that are added in before it hits the pan
can be whatever's in the fridge: cooked veg or chopped-up ham.

Whether it's tortilla that is made or else frittata,
they both work well as snack or lunch, or also as a starter.
They work well warm and also work well later on that day:
room temperature brings out their flavour in a different way.

They work with both a coffee raised and, later, with some beers:
tortillas and frittatas are both there for all the cheers.
They come from different countries but share more than
    what divides,
so take a slice of *both* (before comparing their insides).

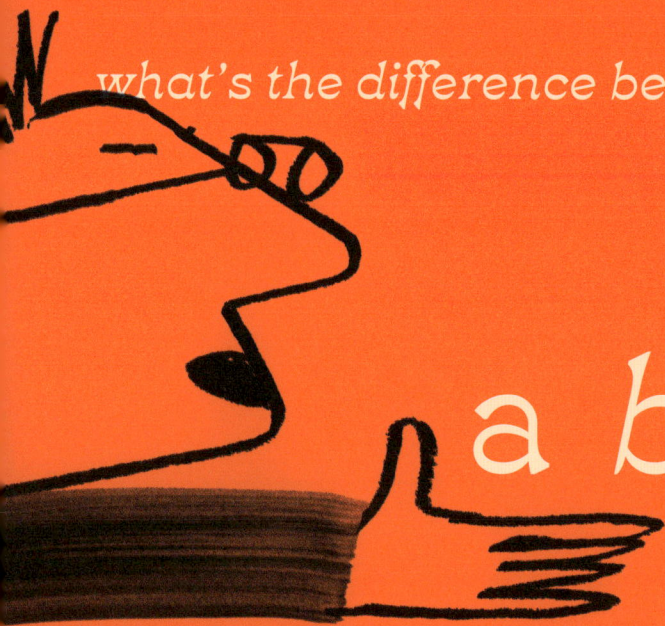

a bun

and

a roll

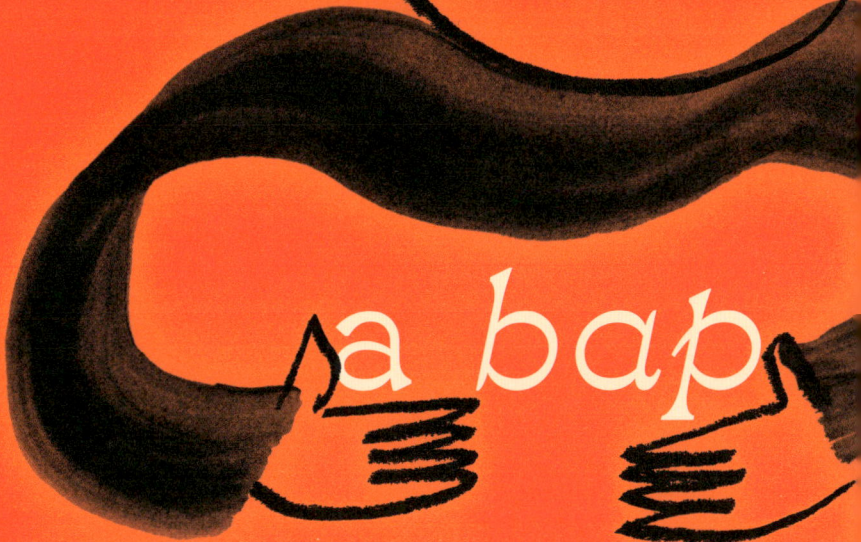

(and

a *bap*

and

a cob)?

They're such a part of daily life, they're known to everyone:
but what is it that makes a roll a roll (and not a bun)?
They're both quite small – opposed to loaves – designed to fit
    the hand,
but slice apart these bready bakes and there's uncertain land.

So… what's a roll?

For land – within the British Isles – here plays a major part,
since where you live determines what you call bread from
    the start.
One simple roll: depending where you are, you'll find a name
that's rooted in a time and place, so no two are the same.

Starting in the south – that's England, southern Wales too –
calling it a 'bread roll' is what most folks tend to do.
Higher up – the Midlands – and a roll is called a 'cob':
in Nottingham and Derby, it's this term that does the job.

A 'crust cob' might be what it's called – so, not a general 'bap' –
though bap's the chosen word, for roll, when heading up the map.
For in the North – in Scotland – then a bap's the common word.
In northern Wales and Staffordshire the term is also heard…

In Coventry and Liverpool, a roll is called a 'batch'.
The name is pretty local to the North-West England patch.
The word's an old Germanic one, evolving from 'to bake',
in Lancashire the word that's used is generally 'barm cake'.

'Barm' is the word that once described the foamy, frothy head,
taken from fermenting ale and used to leaven bread.
It's called a 'cake' but cake it's not: the name refers instead
to categories once given to the different shapes of bread.

With 'bread' the general term for any dough that's baked to rise,
'loaf' or 'cake' were words employed, depending on the size.
A 'loaf' was used for larger bread, a 'cake' for those more small:
the hand-held rolls we think of now, shaped like a little ball.

So this is how a 'barm cake' has its name; we see the term
is used, as well, in 'tea cakes' (that's a roll when in Blackburn).
The eastern half of Lancashire, West Yorkshire, also Leeds,
here 'teacakes' are the rolls the baker makes and bakes
    and kneads.

In Oldham – in North England – it's a 'muffin' that you eat:
a muffin as in bread roll, not the other type that's sweet.
It's not the same as muffins that are cooked flat on the griddle,
the English breakfast muffins that are sliced right through
    the middle.

A 'rowie' is a butter-rich bread roll in Aberdeen.
The butter levels being high, for shelf life will then mean
the rolls can last for days – it's due to this they've come to be
a staple food for fishermen who spend their days at sea.

A 'stottie' in the North-East is a bread roll on the fence.
(It's sitting there as, texture-wise, its filling is more dense.
It's made from bits of off-cut dough: no second knead or rise,
so when it comes to soft bread rolls, these win no
    first-place prize.)

So... what's a bun?

So what a roll is called is not the same for everyone.
In North-East England – Durham, Tyne and Wear – it's called
   a 'bun'.
A bun, that is a soft bread *roll*: a roll that's savoury,
unlike the buns that southerners think buns should tend to be.

A London bun, a Chelsea bun, a hot cross bun: all sweet.
Raisin-filled or icing-glazed: less functional, more treat.
A London bun is finger-shaped: it's longer than it's wide,
and Chelsea buns (and hot cross buns) have currants
   mixed inside.

There's Belgian buns with cherry tops and filled with
   lemon curd,
It turns out bun – like roll – is not a homogenous word.
The dough for all these types of buns – the sweet kind and
   their ilk –
has been enriched so, rather than the water, there is milk.

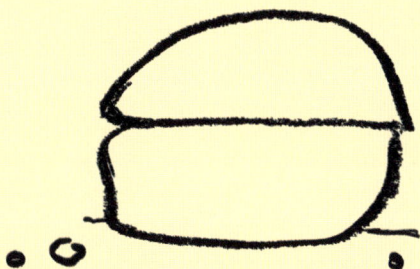

Butter, also sugar, and from there a world of fun,
resulting in all sorts of different kinds of sweetened bun.
Brioche is the way that many burgers want to go:
these buns require a very lengthy kneading of the dough.

Bagels are a dense round bun – enriched (so not a roll) –
distinguished by their chewy crust and by their famous hole.
There is another category of buns that are esteemed –
the ones from South-East Asia that which are filled and
    then get steamed.

Jjinppang buns with red bean paste, *bakpao* filled with
   ground pork;
the range of buns means that we need to ask some questions
   – talk.
For though it's just a little word it can, we see, confuse,
if cited when it's not, in fact, that word that's best to use.

The *point* is that it's not just words: these rolls sat on the shelf
are linked to place and story and a people's sense of self.
So take a moment, use the word that for each place is right.
To give a roll its given due (and sate the appetite).

what's the difference between

a cook

and a chef?

In a restaurant…

Le chef would be insulted if they were to be mistook
for a 'general, common, food-producing, normal, standard cook'.
For chef means 'chief'; it's from the French for *chef de la cuisine*.
So, what does being 'chef' (not 'cook'), within a restaurant, mean?

The difference, in the old-school sense, might seem to be about
the fact that chefs will often be the ones to scream and shout.
For they're in charge – their ego's large – they stand back,
    judge and look
and supervise while all the others chop and prep and cook.

'All the others' are the cooks who constitute their team:
they know their role, they know their place, and what these
    two things mean.
For though a chef's a *type* of cook, the opposite's not true:
for all the many cooks there are, chefs number just a few.

'Yes, chef!' is something you will hear; 'Yes, cook' is never heard.
For cook will have their head down, focused on what's
    being stirred.
For cooks are busy cooking, for it is a doing verb
(which means they can spend hours picking leaves off
    just one herb).

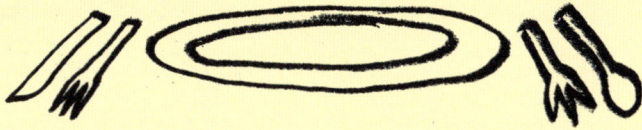

'Cheffing' is, by contrast, not a word you hear in books –
it's not a verb (like cooking is), for chefs don't only cook.
A chef's job is to run the team; their job is to dictate,
while chefs must listen and obey (then slice and stir or grate).

But any talk of one *'chief chef'* does little to include
the number (and the range) of chefs who all make up the food.
There's *'head chef'* and there's 'sous chef' (who's a type
    of deputy),
there's 'station chefs' (who also might be called *chefs de partie*).

The next rung down, we have the guys who have 'cook' in
    their name:
'line cooks', 'prep cooks', 'commis cooks' – they're basically
    the same.
They often start as kitchen porters or as *stage* 'interns',
working hard and fast to hone their skills, they quickly learn.

The more they learn, the higher up the ranks they slowly climb.
The structure is a rigid one, within the world 'fine dine'.
The cooks and chefs who last the course can do tasks on repeat;
the rest should leave the kitchen if they cannot stand the heat.

At home...

We need to look, as well, at what the role is of home cooks:
the ones who love their food and all their oil-stained
  cooking books.
Is what they're doing different? It's still food they've also made,
or is the only difference that they're doing so unpaid?

While chefs are part of one large team, cooks are those based
  at home
who tend to be a one-man band, as they work all alone.
This also means that all the jobs are on them from the start
(unlike those in a team who will just focus on one part).

While chefs will often do one thing in endless repetition,
the cook at home does everything, by just their own volition.
Cooks at home will have more freedom; they can improvise –
while chefs must weigh things out 'just so', home cooks can use
  their eyes.

Chefs make food that needs to have complete consistency.
Home cooks have much more wiggle room for how it comes to be.
'Rustic' is a useful word if things don't *quite* work out,
while for the chef, if plan-A bombs, they may well scream
  and shout.

Chefs think that this is okay, for having a short fuse
is linked, within their minds, to some creative cooking muse.
The home cook, though, will just be thought to have a
   grumpy mood
if they're so shouty when it comes to cooking up some food.

Chefs use fancy language (if in doubt just use the French:
mise en place describes the food-prep, sitting on the bench).
While chefs cook to a menu, home cooks tend to simply 'conjure',
depending on what's in the fridge to satisfy their hunger.

Chefs 'plate up' while cooks will just 'put the food upon the table'.
People help themselves at home because, at home, they're able.
Chefs shout 'service!' when it's ready; home cooks just
   shout 'dinner!'
Cook's just happy supper's made (while chef feels like 'a winner').

Home cooks get to sit straight down with those who are around.
Chefs keep going – service can feel like a battleground.
Home cooks get to raise their glass, delight and draw a breath
as someone makes a lovely toast to celebrate… 'the chef!'

and a Duke of York (etc.)?

With these starchy tubers, there can be a paradox.
For all the many different kinds we see in our veg box:
when it comes to knowing, really, where we should begin,
we struggle to see further than the colour of their skin.

'Red' or 'white' is, by and large, the choice we think to make
(depending on our plan to boil, or roast, or mash, or bake).
But such a colour-coded choice means we are left confused
about the range – and it is *vast!* – that is there to be used.

Rather than just 'red' or 'white', the *season* is the thing,
for what's dug out in winter will be different from the spring.
From spring through early summer (that is May, June and July)
the 'earlies' will get harvested: their water content's high.

This means they have a waxy feel and keep, when cooked,
     their shape.
Which makes them, for a salad, such a perfect choice to make.
The fact that they are small and won't collapse will also mean
they're best when simply boiled or when they're cooked
     by means of steam.

These earlies are called 'new': a name that makes, of course,
    good sense.
And since they have that moisture they will seem quite firm
    and dense.
The starch has not developed, which means, when they're
    met with heat,
there's not a huge conversion (which would end up
    tasting sweet).

These small – and 'new' – potatoes that are picked
    when immature
will always be, for some, the best, the ones that are most 'pure'.
Their taste is somewhat nutty and they perish pretty fast
(they need the starch if they're to be potatoes that will last).

There are the ones called Maris Bard or Pentland Javelin
(Duke of York and Jersey Royal also, here, fit in).
Casablanca, Rocket or a Swift can play the role
of starring in a salad or just steamed and eaten whole.

The 'second earlies' are the next to come out of the ground.
They are still small but tend to be more oval than just round.
These are the Charlotte or La Ratte, or something like Nadine:
they have a waxy texture and their flesh is pale cream.

Neither 'new' nor 'old', these are called 'mids': in their defence,
there's nothing wrong with sitting proudly on the middle fence.
For swinging both directions means that they can play the field:
they hold their shape, when boiled, yet when needs must they
    can yield.

After both these earlies have enjoyed their sunny stay,
the 'main crops' are the next ones up, from autumn through
    till May.
They're ready late in summer, when they have become mature.
The vines are cut or dried; the tubers sit in soil to cure.

Sitting in the soil means that their skin gets tough and strong,
which helps them keep quite well, until the next crop
    comes along.
These are the Coras – oval, large – King Edward's also 'old'
or Maris Piper is the one that is most often sold.

Golden Wonder, Desiree, Kerr's Pink are just a few.
These are potatoes that are different from those young
    and new.
For being longer in the ground, the starch amount is high,
which means that when they cook, their texture is more fine
    and dry.

Because of this, the texture is all fluffy, which will mean
they often welcome being met with butter or some cream.
So here we have our fluffy baked potatoes with crisp skin,
or mash – both light and fluffy – with the fat all whisked right in.

It also makes them great for chips, the reason being that
the starch (which is quite high) prevents absorbing too much fat.
This means they won't be greasy and will minimize the risk
of being soggy (when their only job is to be crisp).

These are the ones to use, as well, to thicken up a soup.
When boiled they will collapse into a soggy sort of gloop.
They also work in chowder, where the texture should be thick.
When mashed for gnocchi, cakes or tarts, they also do the trick.

This is the thing that, with our spuds, will always mean the most:
the one that will determine if it's best to mash or roast.
Will things hold close together or, with heat, will they collapse?
The cell walls: do they stay intact or, with heat, soon relax?

It all comes down to starch, it's here the home cook will
    soon learn –
that those with lots disintegrate and those without stay firm.
Beyond the waxy–floury choice and how it then gets heated,
it's also, then, about the method: how the spud is treated.

With mash, as one example, it's a dish made not one way.
It can be light and fluffy or it can be pomme puree.
The pomme puree is what results from being blitzed when hot:
it ends up all elastic (like a cheesy aligot).

There are those who prefer, instead, to pass it through a ricer,
finding what results to be all fluffy (frankly, nicer!).
They are both different types of mash: it's not one 'best',
    one 'worst':
it's all about how much the starch is broken and dispersed.

It can, then, pay to try things out and not get too obsessed
about the different names and which, for what, will be the best.
Using what's in season, be it 'new' or 'mid' or 'old',
will help much more than if it's Mayan or a Yukon Gold.

So, it's the case – it often is – to have a play around.
To dig about: there are a *lot* of tubers underground.

a pie,

a tart

and a quiche?

We know one when we see one, though it's hard to verbalize
what separates the world of quiche from that of tarts and pies.

A pie

Looking first at pies, a simple summary might be:
'a mix of things that are contained within some cooked pastry.'
The 'mixture' here can be a choice of sweet or savoury things:
the name itself refers, it's said, to what a mag-pie brings.

This is the bird that flies around and scoops up what it seeks.
In terms of pie-world pairing this could be some ham and leeks.
Apple–blackberry, cheese and onion – classics that don't fail.
Spinach–feta, chicken–mushroom, old-school steak and ale.

Pies, at first, were always large but that no longer stands
(think of all those small pork pies designed to fit the hands).
So, if not size, is it about a certain sort of shape?
If pies are meant to just be round, are those that aren't a 'fake'?

Looking at a range of pies, we should not judge so soon:
what about an empanada, with its crescent moon?
Cornish pasties: don't they count? Samosas: just ruled out?
It doesn't seem like size or shape is what a pie's about.

The pastry point, as well, is really something of a hash.
Just think of all the pies whose toppings are made up of mash.
Pies like shepherd's pie, of course, or those filled up with fish:
they are still pies, though pastry-free and cooked within a dish.

It seems our pie summation might have crumbled at the start.
Let's see if we're on firmer ground when summing up a tart...

A tart

A tart is always open with a filling seen, not hid.
Though pies will often have one, tarts will never have a lid.
As well as being 'topless', tarts will also tend to be
baked and flat consisting of a base of short pastry.

The filling can be savoury, the filling can be sweet,
depending on the sort of tart you want to make and eat.
Grated cheese and any green, you really can't go wrong;
treacle, Bakewell, fruit or jam or tarte *avec* citron.

With its tang and filling, which is rich with yellow custard –
tarte citron is often thought to really cut the mustard.
Talk of custard – talk of France – you'd think we're in a niche
but these two things can also be what makes a quiche a quiche.

A quiche

Quiche: a rich baked custard that is cooked within a shell.
Success requires a custard that will wobble really well.
For those who want to eat rich food, this filling is the dream,
the wobble gained from one egg, plus three yolks *and*
   double cream.

If it ends up wobble-free, it's really a non-starter.
Quiche should be more like an omelette or a loose frittata.
It's more about the eggs than cream, the filling is quite light
(unlike a tart where eggs just bind the things inside all tight).

What goes inside a quiche can change but that which has
   most fame
is eggs with chopped-up bacon: it's the classic quiche Lorraine.
Unlike pies and tarts, a quiche, in principle, must be
filled with cheese and things that make it always savoury.

The pastry can be shortcrust, or some flaky or rough puff.
Either way, it has a 'give': no pastry should be tough.
Making it from scratch, all things must be kept very cold
and don't forget it can be bought: pre-made and ready-rolled.

This shortcut might well mean that this will then incentivize
the making of all sorts of quiche and tarts and *also* pies.
As you roll and fill and bake and hone the pastry art
there will be lots of time to ponder: 'quiche' or 'pie' or 'tart'?

what's the difference between

a sausage and

a frankfurter?

Sausages are, typically, a mix of chopped-up meat.
There are, though, lots of different kinds that people like to eat.
This makes them hard to bundle up and neatly classify,
but being hard is not a reason for us not to try.

There are three major groups so 1, 2, 3 is where we start.
'Fresh' is one, next 'cured', then 'cooked' (or sometimes 'cooked
    in part').
Looking at these three, in turn: a run through of this list
will give a sense of *quite* how many sausages exist.

The first up of these groups is 'fresh', these sausages come raw.
In order to be eaten they must be cooked through before.
The meat is unfermented so these bangers will not last;
their journey from the butcher to the hot pan should be fast…

Once you've got your meat and fat and salt, there's room to play,
for sausages can be spiced up – there's more than one set way.
Different British regions have a sausage linked to home:
a certain set of spices for which they are then well known.

They all include black pepper, and ground mace is quite the rage.
Lots of them will also have some earthy, musky sage.
Nutmeg, ginger, cloves, cayenne: these are the chosen spice
that lots of regions like to make their sausages taste nice.

Pork can be the only meat or sometimes paired with veal.
Most are mixed with rusk crumb or a bit of sausage meal.
The more proportion meat-to-meal, the 'better' it will be
(if 'better' is defined as meat, which is deemed 'quality').

That's just Britain, there – of course – will also always be
all the different kinds that can be found across the sea.
Germany is number one – the mighty sausage reigns.
France, as well, and Italy and Portugal and Spain.

These countries have their share of fresh, but also love
   them cured:
this is our second group where, first, the fresh meat is matured.
Smoked or dried or salted, this will all affect the taste;
regardless of the choice of cure, it's never done in haste.

Once it's cured and seen as ready, packed up and then priced:
these have a shelf life that is long, as they wait to be sliced.
Italy, for instance, has a range that is quite wide –
salame crudo is the name for meat not cooked, just dried.

Sausages can also be so soft that they get spread,
like Spanish *sobrasada* (that's the one that is quite red).
Teewurst is the German kind: a finely textured paste
made from pork (or beef and pork) and highly spiced to taste.

Sausages, in Germany, are something of an art –
just one of which is those that are all-cooked (or cooked-in-part).
It's here, within this group (the one that we have deemed
   as third)
That 'frankfurter''s the name that will be very often heard.

The thing that makes a frankfurter so loved and highly prized
is the texture, which results from being liquidized.
It's blitzed up with its own fats like a sauce emulsified,
and there's something called saltpetre that then brings
   a bright pink dye.

The batter is cohesive so the casing gets removed.
It's the test upon which all the best frankfurters get approved.
For this means that a frank will snap and 'if no snap, no point'!
(says every self-respecting, hot-dog-loving selling joint).

Franks are also known as Wienies; they are both the same.
They are a product of the place (which is seen in their name).
How they get to 'hot dog' from that point is not so clear
but links with dachshund 'sausage dogs' at some point
   did appear.

So that's a little summary of several sausage types.
Meat, first ground then bound and shaped in tubular-like pipes.
Choose your topping, sauce or side: whichever works is great
(though what should pair with what is 'frank-ly' one whole
   new debate...!)

...and what's the difference between a 'corn dog' and a 'K-dog'?

First up is a 'corn dog', where the USP, the trick,
is skewering the sausage with a thin, long, wooden stick.
From here it is then coated in a batter of cornmeal,
deep-fried and eaten (at a fairground for the real deal).

Korean corn dogs are the same, though they prefer rice flour
and many love the 'K-dog' for its filling-topping power.
Stringy mozzarella is the standard choice, the treat.
The dog is fried then eaten, like a lolly, on the street.

what's the difference between

a pumpkin

and a

squash?

The family tree for 'squash' is vast, within it you will find
a multitude of names, of which 'pumpkin' is just one kind.
For there are species that are made distinctive for the reason
that they are grown in separate continents and also season.

Asia is where lots of squash will think of as their home.
Africa, as well, is where these species can be grown.
These are the watermelons and the gourds with their
  thick skins;
melons, too, and cucumbers (and also small gherkins).

The other major group of squash are grown within the States.
The group is massive, so it's here that one will find 'the greats'.
The butternut is quite the favourite: it's the squash *du jour*
but there, in fact, are *lists* of squash: there are so many more.

Crown Prince and turban, mini-munchkin: no two look the same.
They look, in fact, as you imagine from their given name.
Grey ghost, for instance, is as spooky as its name would seem,
its skin is almost see-through with its pale and greyish green.

The US group is split in two – the split itself is neat.
There's 'winter squash' (which is mature) and 'summer squash'
  (less sweet).
The skin is thick on winter squash; this gives a long shelf life,
but also means it can be hard to slice up with a knife.

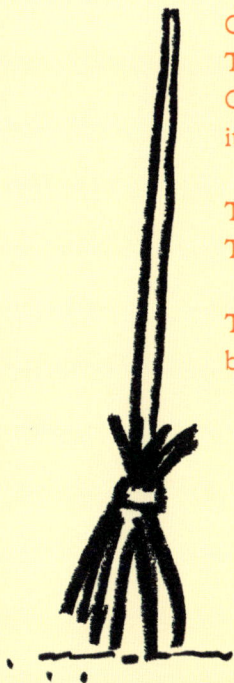

But though the preparation of this squash can take a while,
once you're in – and seeds are scooped – the flesh is versatile.
Being firm means when it's cooked it's generally robust:
as happy to be roasted, boiled, mashed – it's not too fussed.

The flavour of the flesh, when cooked, is chestnut-ty and sweet.
This is the best of autumn food; not just for trick or treat.
For though the pumpkins grown to carve are great
   for Halloween,
these Jack O' Lantern pumpkins are best hollow, lit – just *seen*.

For when it comes to actual *taste*, these aren't the ones to use:
acorn, hubbard, red kuri are more the ones to choose.
From there it's soup or pie or stew or mash as ways to go,
paired with sage or lemon, cream or chilli and miso.

Summer squash, by contrast, are a very different set.
Headed up by green or yellow zucchini/courgette.
(Zucchini is the US name – they look to Italy);
the UK takes its lead from France, hence 'courgette' came to be.)

Because it's less mature, the summer squash flesh is less sweet.
It softens when it cooks so it is delicate to eat.
It works as well when eaten raw: a shaved ribbon or slice
(when paired with feta, rocket, dill) is *really* rather nice.

Mixing up the yellow and the green squash (if you can)
looks great, or try to find the yellow squash called pattypan.
This has a funky spaceship shape, it's eaten skin and all;
the stuff of Cinderella's dreams in getting to that ball.

Crookneck squash is, as it sounds, long with a neck
   that's curved.
While marrow's size reflects the extra plant time it has served.
Its size means there's more water, and more water equals 'wet'.
so marrow's will be mild in taste, compared to a courgette.

As with other summer squash, when cooked it loses shape.
So this can predetermine what you can and want to make.
The texture of each squash is what will single each one out
in terms of what the difference is – this is what it's about.

Luckily for those who want to eat squash all year round,
there is the right and perfect squash to be grown, bought
   or found.
Some are honey-sweet while others taste more like a nut.
So play around with different kinds: don't get 'squashed'
   in a rut!

what's the difference between

pasta

and noodles?

Pasta comes from Italy – the word means 'paste' or 'dough'.
Noodle's from the German *Nudel* (not Marco Polo!
For though he's often credited with 'finding' them in China,
his noodle role in Europe, it turns out, was rather minor).

Looking at ingredients, the difference is quite neat:
true pasta is just made from semolina durum wheat.
Durum wheat is hard and coarser than all other flour –
it's this that brings it real strength (and robust Roman power).

Its gluten content's high and strong: its fans are fully hooked
upon this grain paste, which is strong and won't collapse
    when cooked.
It's best to cook *al dente* so it has a little bite,
for pasta that is overcooked is not considered right.

Noodles, on the other hand, are milled from common wheat.
It's softer than the pasta flour, so less robust with heat.
Because of this, in with the noodles you will always find
salt added to the raw dough, as it's this which makes it bind.

Can you tell a King Edward from a Duke of York?
Or pick a Parmesan from a pecorino?

In these 30 rhymes, Tara imparts years of cooking to solve all your culinary conundrums in a way that is accessible, witty and – most of all – fun.

Playful riffs on etymology, Anglo-American cultural differences lost in translation, and the subtle differences between products and ingredients feature throughout, teaching us about where our food came from, and why we call it that, and ultimately celebrating how food brings us together.

"A collection that will earn its place on kitchen shelves long after most of its glossy contemporaries have been replaced by newer models." Felicity Cloake

As the in-house writer of Team Ottolenghi over the last decade **Tara Wigley** has co-written eight major books, including million-selling *Ottolenghi, Simple* and *Falastin*. She is also the author of *How To Butter Toast* (Pavilion).

In addition, she writes the weekly Ottolenghi *Guardian* column and the monthly column in the *New York Times*. She has a dedicated following on Instagram and writes about food in ways that audiences find engaging and informative.

She was a judge on the 2022 Fortnum & Mason Food & Drink awards.

For publicity requests, please contact:
komal.patel@harpercollins.co.uk

HarperCollins *Publishers*

So unlike with the pasta where it's just there for the taste,
salt really helps the structure of the basic noodle paste.
As pasta dough requires no salt it goes into the pot
of water, which is salted well (here 'well' means quite a *lot*).

Another way the difference of the two can be explained
is looking at the quantity of egg the dough contains.
Though pasta dough can have some egg, the noodle dough
   is *meant*
to have a minimum amount of 5.5 per cent.

Noodles also differ in the fact that they can be
made from a range of foods of such great, vast diversity.
Some are starch, these are the ones called 'glass' or 'cellophane'
(the Japanese translation has the meaning of 'spring rain')

Sweet potato also works, and buckwheat has some fame –
for those who want things gluten-free, then 'soba' is the name.
Mung bean or rice, these tasty choices both can hit the spot
for those who want some noodles for the free-from foodie lot.

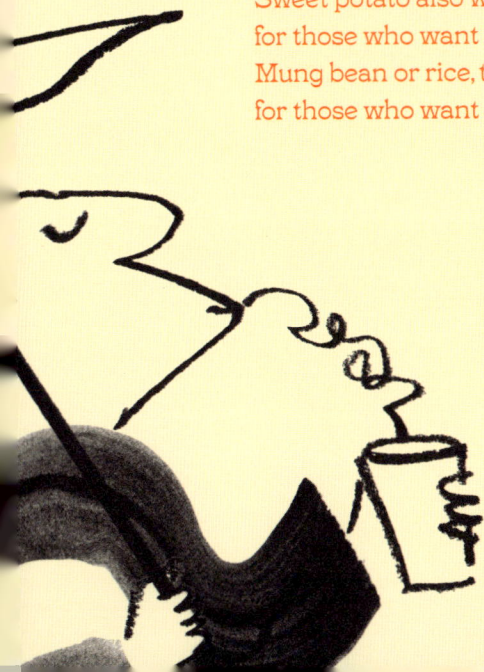

If what is *in* them is the clearest difference we can test,
the next is looking at the different ways they get processed.
The difference here is cut and dried (the pun means
   no confusion:
for though they are both cut and dried, the pasta's
   from *extrusion*).

Extrusion is like squeezing toothpaste out of great long tubes;
malleable so it can form all types of lengths and cubes.
The semolina–water paste gets pushed through one large 'die'.
This is the mould whose many shapes explain, in turn, the why:
the why and how of pasta taking on so many shapes
is that it's moulded by the shape the die is set to make.

Noodles, unlike pasta, tend to be more uniform –
strands, like ribbons, stemming from the 'roll-cut' way
   they're born.
The dough is rolled out really flat into a long, thin sheet
before it's cut – the choice is thick or thin but always neat.

Another way they differ, once they have been dried and aired
is how they're served and what the sauce is with which they
    get paired.
Because of pasta's texture (which is firm and strong and coarse)
it's often served with different types of textured pasta sauce.

What sauce gets made depends upon the pasta's size
    and shape.
This will dictate the thickness of the sauce that it can take.
Tubes with ridges, for example (those you see right through),
like a chunky veggie sauce or meaty, thick ragu.
Something like spaghetti, though, can't hold a sauce so tight,
so it will find a silky smooth tomato sauce just right.

Pasta *needing* sauce, however, is not automatic.
It comes in broth or soup; no pairing is axiomatic.
It's just the same with noodles, where it would incite hot wrath
to say that noodles always come along in bowls of broth.

Their texture means, though, it is true, that broth will often be
the perfect pairing for the noodles when they're slippery.
The difference, though, is slippery: it's not an *either/or.*
They can come with a dipping sauce, or with a soup you pour.

There's much to say upon this matter, books to fill a school,
for every statement has, of course, exceptions to the rule.
So heap your plates and fill your bowls: read more, ask more
    and talk
(and question why you're holding chopsticks, or a spoon
    and fork...)

what's the difference between

one
(dried)
chilli

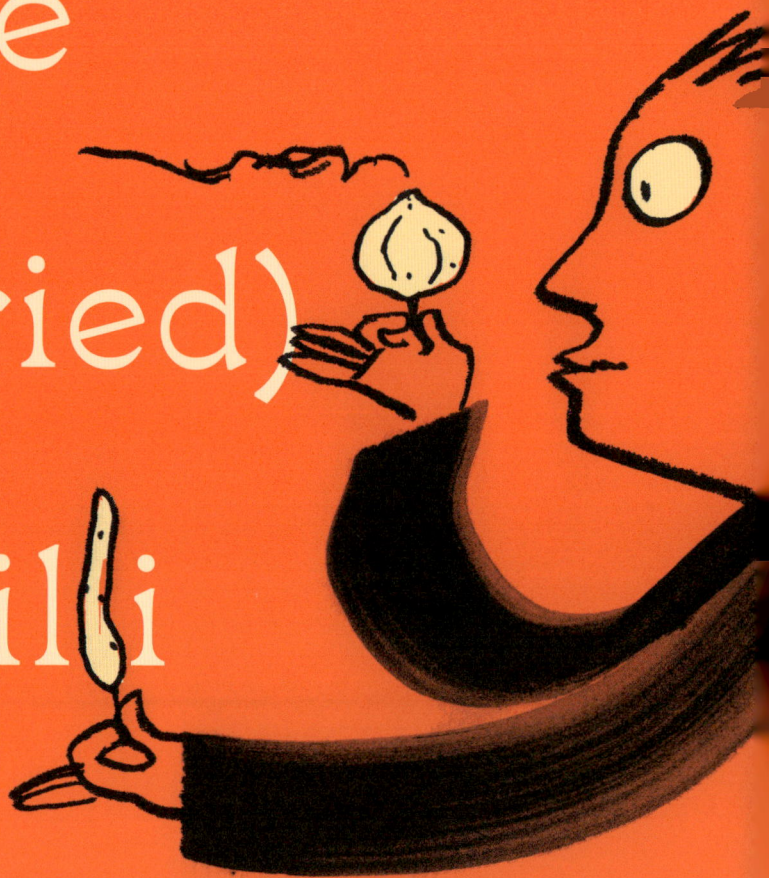

and

another?

Chillies can be mouth-burn hot, or they can be quite mild.
They can feel like a great, warm hug or else an angry child.
Since listing all the different kinds would fill a major book,
let's look, instead, at five with which it's really nice to cook.

First, we have Aleppo flakes, from Turkey, mild in heat.
Their colour is bright burgundy, their flavour almost sweet.
Because they're really gentle, you can sprinkle as you wish:
they work on eggs and roasted veg and hummus, meat
    and fish.

From Mexico, we have ancho: these are poblanos, dried.
Their name describes their look as *ancho* means, in
    English, 'wide'.
Their heat is very mild, there are notes of rich, ripe fruit;
there's talk of tasting (in a good way) like a leather boot.
Add one to some tomatoes that are cooking, deep and red
(and if you don't have ancho, use smoked paprika instead).

From Central Mexico, there is a round one: cascabel.
Its name, in Spanish, translates nicely: it means 'little bell'.
It's how it looks and how it sounds: the name itself is taken,
from how the seeds can make a noise inside when it is shaken.
Add it to a soup or stew: it's chocolate-like (not hot)
and brings a fruity–woody note once added to the pot.

Chipotle chilli is another kind from Mexico.
This is a jalapeno when it's fresh (which some don't know).
It then gets smoked and dried out, which then makes it
    lose its heat.
It's gentle and it's smoky-rich: it tastes a bit like meat.
It works in soups and sauces, but it also is dessert.
Trying adding some to chocolate: you will see it doesn't hurt!

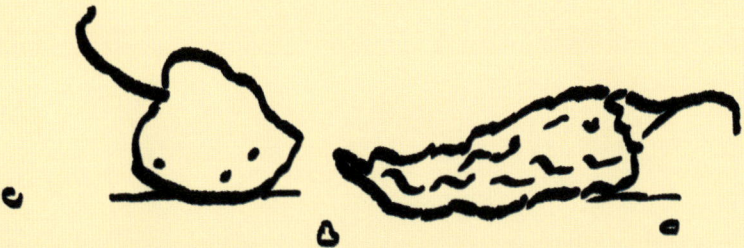

Last up, try out some Urfa flakes: they're Turkish, crimson-black.
They make eggs looks so great they almost feel like a hack.
They're striking and they're pretty when they're sprinkled
   on a plate.
Fish or meat or leaves, once Urfa-ed: they all look so great.
Their taste is mild and earthy and their heat is nice and low;
add them to some butter and divine is where you go.

So that's a little intro, chillies: one, two, three, four, five.
Seek them out and play around: your taste buds *will* survive!

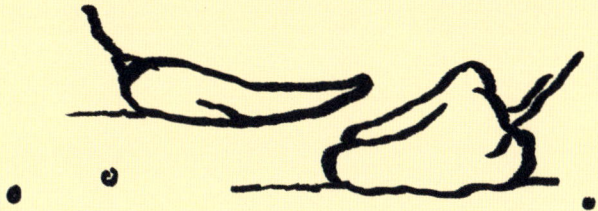

what's the difference between

a Nigel and

a Nigella?

First, Nigella is 'NIGELLA!'; she is, frankly, just the queen!
Nigel's Mr 'Nigel Slater', he's a little more serene.
His vibe and food and life and house, there is a tranquil poise;
Nigella tends towards the camp – her food makes much
   more noise!

Her gammon's braised in Coca-Cola, celebrating kitsch.
Her peanut butter chocolate cake has *four* tiers (yes, it's rich!).
The fairy lights are dancing and her counter's quite the riot.
With Nigel, it is *less is more*; it's much more still and quiet.

He's one to be inspired by a single piece of fruit.
He takes you to its essence on a lovely, gentle route.
His recipes help with the single squash sat in the drawer;
he'll bring it back to sumptuous life and then his 'twist' adds more.

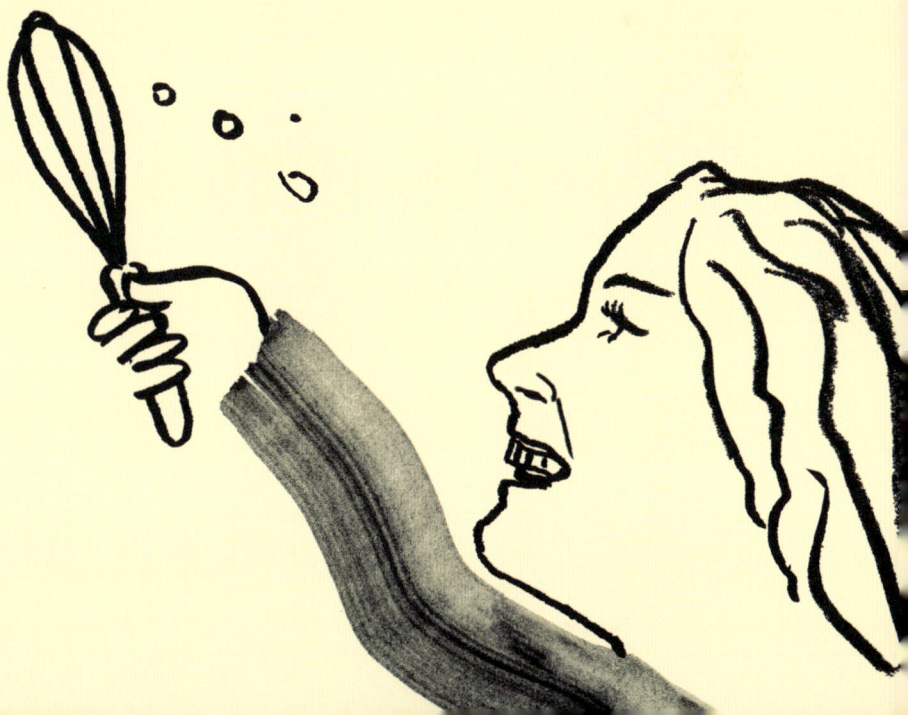

He'll reach for toasted pumpkin seeds, he'll pull apart burrata;
he'll transform it from 'just a squash' into a stunning starter.
He'll write it up in such a way that for a while you'll be
part of the Nigel Slater world, enthralled by poetry.

The fact Nigella's name is shared with black nigella seeds
is just so great for someone who both cooks and also feeds.
And though it's just by chance the seeds go by Nigella's name,
there's not *such* heft in 'Nigel seeds': they don't sound quite
   the same.

Nigel, though, has something to his name that he can boast:
the claim to avocado smashed and spread upon hot toast.
Though hard, of course, to pinpoint, there are many who
   will credit
the 'recipe' to Nigel as the one who wrote and said it.

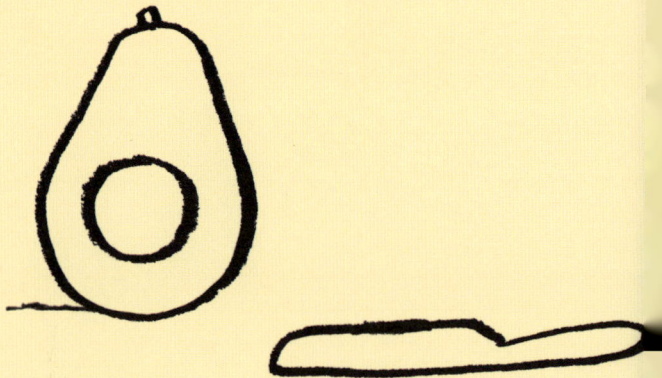

Nigella is a writer, first – it's really how she writes,
that she shares with us her love of food; of stirs and sips
    and bites.
Her writing style is intimate: it conjures up a home,
as though she's speaking to a friend or reader on the phone.

Nigel was a trained 'chef' first but then became a 'cook'.
A cook who writes (and *really* writes: he's on his
    nineteenth book).
It's the cooking *and* the writing and the ease with which
    they're done
that puts *both* on a pedestal – loved by everyone.

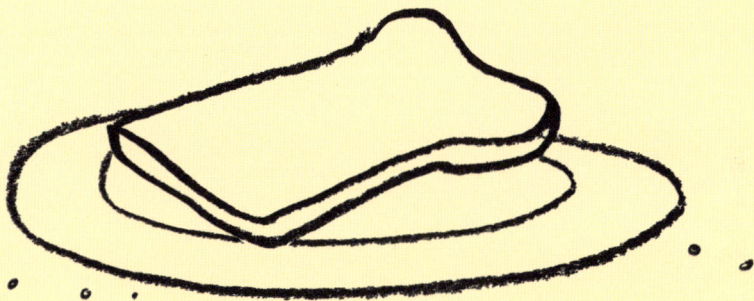

what's the difference between an

eggplant

and

an aubergine?

An 'appetizer', in the States, is how a meal commences.
Calling it an 'entree' is confusing to the senses.
For an 'entree' is the main course, where the person eating gets
clean, shiny 'flatware' ('knife and fork') and 'napkin' ('serviette').

If the 'server' (that's the 'waiter') asks if they can 'help you out',
then the guest should say "sure thing" ("yes, please") to
    minimize the doubt.
For if British diners ask for 'chips', for instance, there's a risk
that what comes, if eating in the States, is just a bowl of crisps.

If what's wanted is some 'crisps' (to have alongside snacks
    and dips)
then what needs to be requested is, instead, 'potato chips'.
And if long, thin 'chips' are wanted then these must be called
    'French fries'
(though in Britain it's a 'chip': for any shape, or length, or size).

It's not only sorting out a fry from chip or thick-cut wedge.
The confusion can arise with so much other fruit and veg.
If a Brit is in the States and asks if there's some 'aubergine'
then the server might well say 'I'm sorry, what is that
    you mean?'

'Oh, it's eggplant that you want – okay – it's eggplant that
    you'll get.
And I trust you mean "zucchini" when you talk about "courgette".'
And your green and yellow 'peppers', in the States, are known
    as 'bell',
and most green leaves go by different names (of course they
    do!) as well.

If a punchy 'rocket' salad is the order of the day,
it's 'arugula' that, in the States, one needs to learn to say.
What a Brit will call 'cos lettuce' is American 'romaine':
it's confusing when two different words mean, actually,
    the same.

Though both countries have the green and white and
    pepper-tasting allium,
the US break it down into 'spring onion' and 'scallion'.
The former has the big and bulbous, spherical white base,
while the latter is the thin one with the stronger,
    less-sweet taste.

And 'cilantro', in the States, is 'coriander' (though when dried,
it's called 'coriander': in this case, there is no word divide.)
It's not only fruit and veg where terminology is trying;
in the butchers, it's the same for those perusing, and then buying.

For when the Brits refer to 'braising steak', this is the same
    as 'chuck'.
And if asking for a 'cutlet', then a Brit will have no luck.
And a 'fillet steak', for Brits, is for the US 'tenderloin',
and a 'porterhouse' is composite – the cut where two parts join.

If what's wanted is some 'minced beef', in the US ask for 'ground'.
And remember, in the States, the weights are ounces,
    also pounds!
And one US quart (for liquid) is one UK (metric) litre,
and three feet, if in the US, is around about a metre.
And one metre (in the UK) is just longer than a yard.
It seems sharing words and language seems to make things,
    in fact, *hard!*

How we cook, in what

And it's, sadly, not just what we cook: it's how we cook, in what –
and one person's choice Dutch oven, in the UK is a 'pot'.
And a sheet pan is the one that's flat, upon which cookies bake,
while a 'baking pan' is needed if it's savoury to make.

In the US, it's a 'skillet', in the UK 'frying pan'.
In the UK it's a 'tin' and in the US it's a 'can'.
It's a 'can', as well, to name what, in the US, trash goes in.
For the Brits this is referred to not as trash but 'rubbish bin'.

In the UK, mention 'cup' and thoughts will be of teatime pleasure
whereas, in the States, a cup is used to weigh out, and to measure.
And the weight, in grams, will change depending what is in the cup
(so, a Brit should be advised to simply look conversions up).

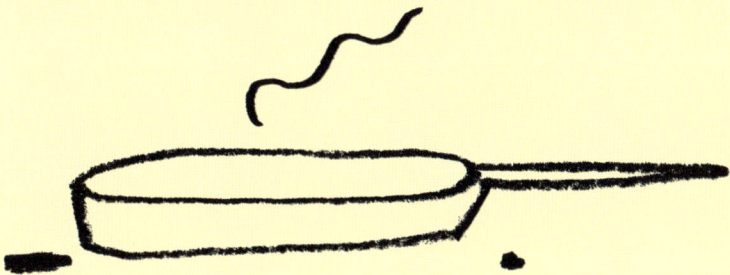

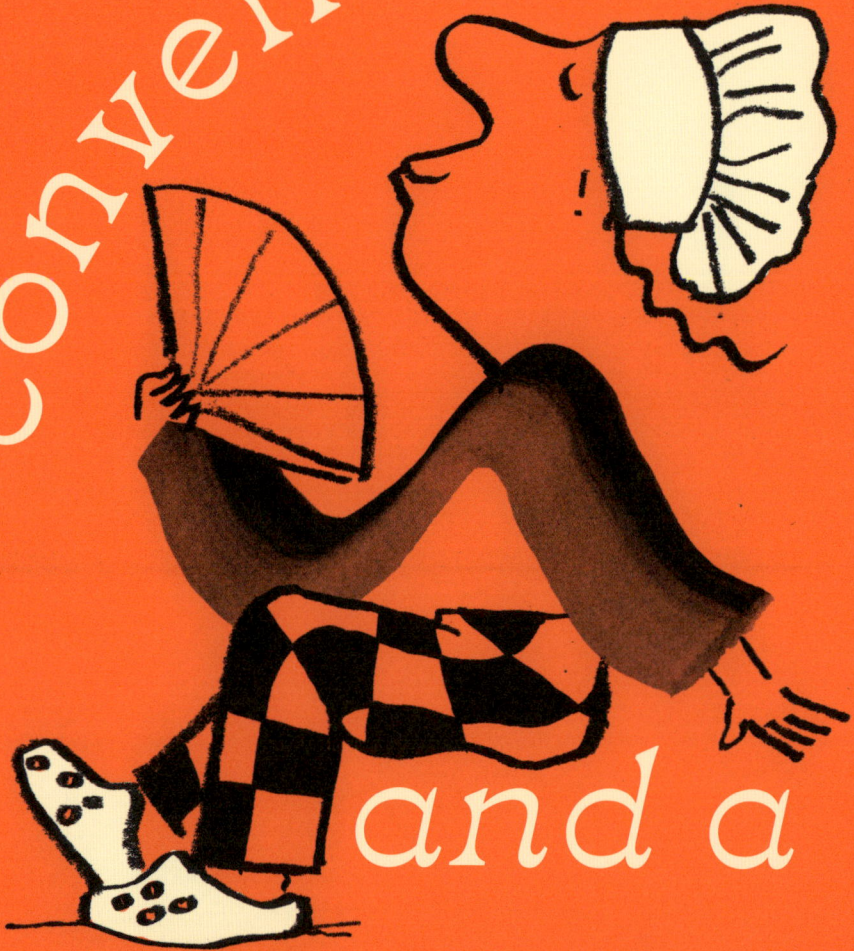

what's the difference between a

conventional

and a

fan oven?

Knowing what these are (and aren't) is useful, for they govern
the way that food gets baked and cooked once it's inside
  our oven.

Convention (or conventional): the cook, in this case, sets
the oven to a temperature to which, therefore, it gets.
There's just one source of heat inside: it rises from below.
It's all quite plain and simple: there's not much more to know.

Inside an oven with a fan, a fan is always found.
It has the job of helping move the hot air round and round.
The heat inside is even – with convention there's a spot
that can either be too cool or, on the other hand, too hot.

It's these spots that mean a cook must think to check and,
    maybe, turn
any tray inside the oven so what's on them will not burn.
It's convention, though, will tend to be the baker's oven choice,
for what is baked will not dry out and stays a bit more moist.

For with a fan, as we have said, the hot air moves about.
The heat can be intense, which makes what's being baked
  dry out.
If mainly used to bake things that will need to get a rise,
conventional (not fan) might be the oven choice most wise.

Unless, of course, what's wanted is a crispy, crackled crust.
In which case a blast of fan will be a win: a total must!
For anyone who likes their chicken with a crispy skin,
an oven with a fan is where all birds should settle in.

Regardless of the oven, cooks should listen to their hunch,
for common sense is often what will make a well-cooked lunch.
However flash and fancy is the oven that you've got,
it still makes sense to think in terms of 'low' or 'mid' or 'hot'.

For all the research done and all the money that is spent,
each oven – like each cook – has its own quirky temperament.
So don't obsess about the type or if it's old or new:
just spend some time together – get to know it and, it, you.

What's that thing about C20 degrees?!

If when scanning recipes, the home cook reads and sees
a temperature that's set to be two-hundred (fan) degrees,
adjusting to conventional means raising to two-twenty
(some say to go a little more but, really, twenty's plenty).

If written as conventional, then fan goes twenty lower
(the hot air moving round, in fan, means that it will cool slower).
It should be said, most things we bake are really not too fussed.
Just have a peek, when halfway through, and –
    if needs be – adjust.

And what about the difference between convention and convection?!

Another thing that needs a little thought and some inspection
is what the difference is between convention and *convection*.
The words can be confused – they are the same but for
   one letter –
but it's not a case of either/or (or even one that's better).

For convection is a setting (not an oven): it's the heat
that a fan creates when it's switched on for something crisp
   to eat.
So the setting, when it's switched on, makes the oven
   'fan-assisted':
it's another name for which this type of oven can be listed.

So, convection is an option that is either used or not.
It is great for when what's needed is a great, big boost of 'hot'.
The fact that it can either be switched on or not, depending,
means, for those who want both options, it is money well
   worth spending.

what's the difference between

Celsius and

Fahrenheit?

Something that the home cook needs to make sure they
    get right
is the fact that Celsius is not the same as Fahrenheit.
No, they are entirely different, both responding to the ways
that the temperature was measured back in eighteenth-
    century days.

First, Fahrenheit – created by a German man who mused
that a mix of salt and water, with some ice, was good to use.
It was in this mix that zero was decreed and allocated
to the mix from which thermometers were always calibrated.

For, as salt takes down the point at which a liquid will
    then freeze,
so the freezing point was set at minus 32 degrees.
From there, the boiling point was set at 2-1-2 to mean
that the difference (of 180) was a range quite clear and 'clean'.

Two Swedish chaps, two decades on, then raised their hand
     to say,
'Well, we'd like to measure temperature a slightly different way.
For the way we are all working now just feels a little strange,
so we'd like to pose a rounder number for the boil–freeze range.

If we choose to start with zero as the point where "freeze"
     is made,
we can take 100 steps to boil and call it "centi-grade".'
Though the two ways both exist, these days, it never tends
     to hurt
to know both – just to understand – the way they each convert.

The maths bit

So, from Celsius to Fahrenheit, the maths you need to do,
is to multiply by 1.8, then add on 32.
Though a simpler way of doing this (although it looks
   quite long)
is divide by 5 and times by 9, then 32 adds on.
So, for Fahrenheit to Celsius it's opposite this time.
Simply take away the 32, times 5, divide by 9.

There is the option there for those who simply want to cook
to ditch the maths and look it up online or in a book.
For cooking should not feel like maths – there are good
   ways to tell
if something's ready, it is often seen in look or smell.
The oven settings and the numbers are a useful guide,
but to really know what's going on… you need to look inside!

what's the difference between

high tea

and

afternoon tea?

'Pop on over, won't you, for a lovely cup of tea?'
The invite sounds so innocent; so pure and trouble-free.
But don't be duped! One's understanding of the word itself
says much about one's background, social status, class
    and wealth.

For some will think of 'tea' as being scones with cream and jam.
For others it's their main meal: chips and beans and
    sliced-up ham.
The first one's 'afternoon tea', and the latter's known as 'high':
we need to look a few years back to shed some light on why.

Though drinking tea and snacking both took place; they were
    not new,
the practice wasn't widespread until 1842.
The Duke of Bedford's wife – her name was Anna – voiced
    her thinking,
that in the afternoon her stomach felt like it was 'sinking'.

'For lunch is very light and dinner isn't served till eight,
and I, for one, am peckish: this is far too long to wait.'
So when the clock struck four, she'd ask for cake and have
    some tea.
With time, she thought it would be nice to add some company.

What started off as casual, sitting 'round on parlour chairs,
soon came to be frequented by the rich, with all their airs.
And from a snack it came to be a thing on three-tiered stands,
attracting certain types with time upon their (dainty) hands.

So this was 'afternoon tea' – Duchess Anna quickly found
that 'tea' could be a whole new peg to hang the day around.
The fact this tea was served on chairs and tables that were low,
meant 'low tea' was another name by which this tea would go.

With 'low tea' as the 'high class' one, it's clear to then see why,
the 'other one' – the worker's one – was called, by contrast, 'high'.
Though 'high tea' seems the posh one, it's in fact the other way:
the meal that working men would eat once through their
    working day.

The name describes the type of chairs upon which people sat:
the high-backed chairs (not parlour chairs) – the
    explanation's that!
High tea was eaten early, so that everyone was fed:
the table high with hot pork pies or treats like raisin bread.

Cold cuts and pickles, sardines, crumpets served all nice
    and hot.
Tea in hand, which kept on flowing from the central pot.
Today this is called 'dinner' but it just as well can be
referred to, by a lot of folks, as what they have for 'tea'.

If tea is in the evening, then it's dinner at midday,
for those who call that lunch then it's around the other way.
Lunch, then tea, then dinner; it's a minefield if you get
confused regarding which is which and what's the etiquette.

It's all a nonsense, really: who cares what the Joneses think,
It's just a get-together with a cup of tea to drink.
And if you go for 'dinner' and are faced with piles of cake,
there are, most would agree, far worse mistakes that you
    could make.

Debrett's on the matter

There are a lot of rules Debrett's has views on what to do:
'Lavatory' or 'toilet', 'bathroom', 'ladies' or just 'loo'?
Is it 'lunch' or 'dinner', 'scones' or 'shrimps' that we will eat?
Is it called a 'pudding' or 'dessert' or simply 'sweet'.

'Stirring tea: go back and forth (not 'round and 'round and 'round:
this makes the most uncouth and noisy spoon-on-china sound).
You break up scones with fingers; serviettes are not to be;
and it is called a sofa, don't you know: it's not "settee".'

Fictional tea parties...

Imagine *Downton Abbey* if 'The Tiger' came to tea
(now that's a clash of tea times' it would be great fun to see!).

Or *Downton*'s Countess Grantham taking tea in Wonderland
(finding both the Hare and Hatter hard to understand).

Enid Blyton's toffee shocks, pop biscuits – tea of dreams,
or Harry Potter's chocolate frogs and every-flavoured beans.

While all these sound like parties that are set a world apart
they share a link with 'tea time' as conceived right from
 the start.

For all their local colour, at its heart this simple brew
says 'let us have a catch up: you with me and me with you'.

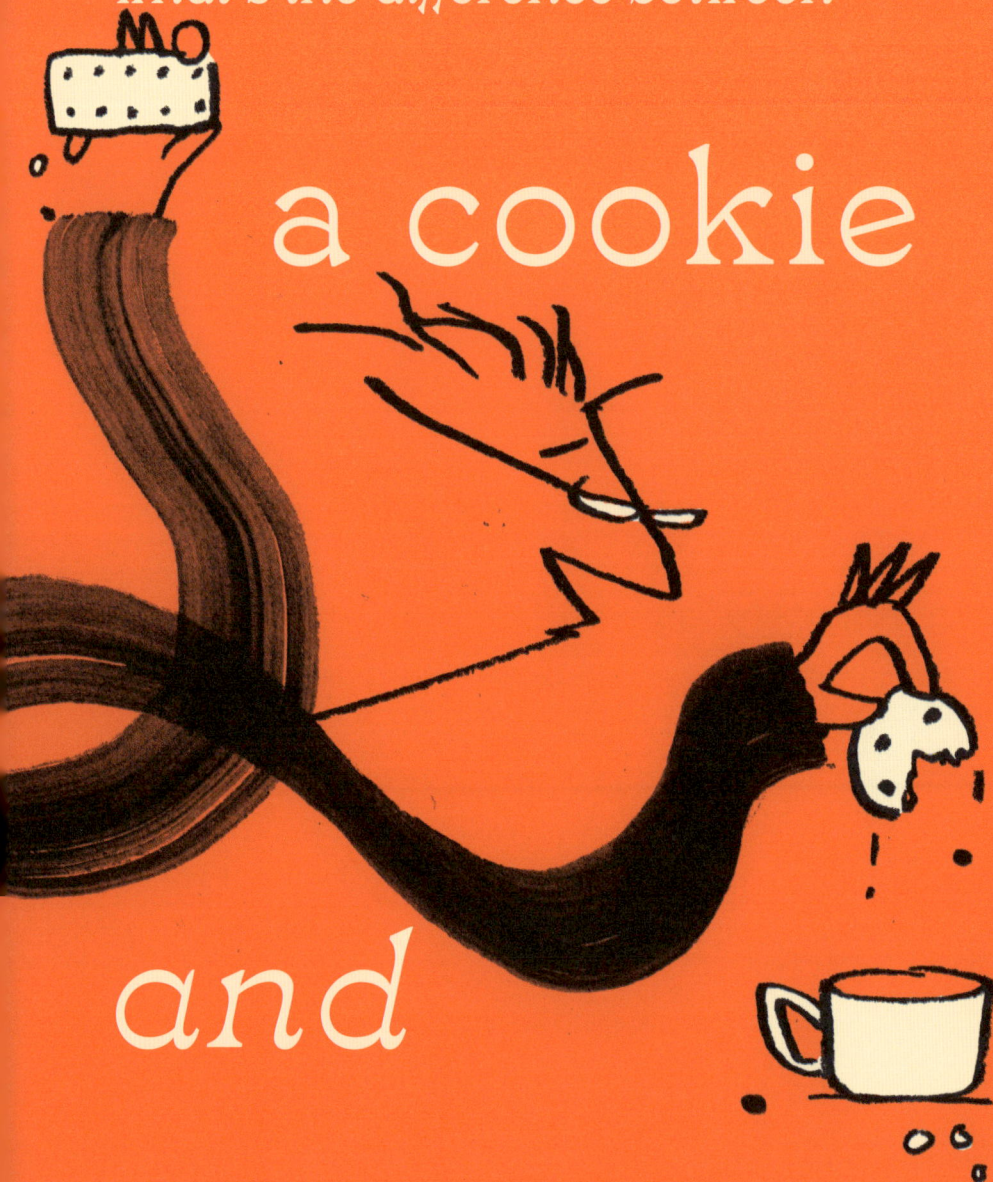

what's the difference between

a cookie

and

a biscuit?

Definitions vary; it's a brave soul who will risk it
and sum up how a cookie is a cookie (not a biscuit).
Aren't they simply baked treats that are eaten with some tea?
Sweet and small – how different, really, can they ever be?

The first bite being with the eye, a good place to begin
is how they look: with cookies being thick (and biscuits thin).
Biscuits, when they snap, will do so with a clean-ish break,
while cookies tend to crumble (as they are a *type* of cake).

Another clear distinction is that cookies will be sweet.
While biscuits can be savoury as well, they're both a treat.
As well as being Hobnobs, Bourbons, Kit Kats (as you please),
biscuits can be plain, with oats, to form a base for cheese.

Some biscuits can be plain, just held together with some cream.
Sticky jam or chocolate spread, these bind the biscuit team.
Think Jammie Dodgers, Custard Creams or classic Oreos,
inside of which the jam or cream or chocolate always goes.

Some will pick a Penguin for a chocolate biscuit bar.
While others think that filling *plus* a coating goes too far.
This is just tea and biscuits, though, a safe and gentle space.
There's room for every type of bake to have a welcome place.

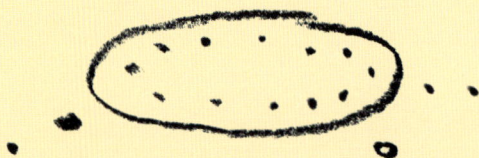

Why is a cookie called a cookie and a biscuit called a biscuit?

The word for cookie is a version of the word in Dutch.
Saying it out loud – *koekje* – might not help all that much.
But change it into English and the word means 'little cake'
and these, indeed, were first conceived of as the 'test run bake'.

The name for biscuits is not Dutch: it's in the Latin book.
From where we see that *bis* means 'twice' and *coquere* means
  'to cook'.
Twice-cooked they are (or were at first), hence being crisp
  and thin,
lasting longer than the cookies in the biscuit tin.

To dunk or not to dunk?

To dunk or not: the subject of the biggest, strong debates.
A topic that can – truly, fully – open all floodgates.
Some will think it's meant to be, while others find it rude,
Thinking it is tantamount to liquefying food.

what's the difference between a

macaroon

and a

macaron?

It is something that we think we get, but do we always know
which is which (and what's the one that has the extra 'o').
For though they look quite different, it is easy to go wrong;
to confuse a mac-a-roon with what is really mac-a-ron.

In terms of what goes in them, there are a lot of things they share:
ground almonds, sugar, egg whites (which are whipped with
   lots of air).
There is never any flour so they're fragile and will be
light (and loved by those who want their sweet treats to be
   gluten-free).

The difference is (and here we hope the macaroons won't mind)
that macarons are chic and fancy: *slightly* more refined.
They're sandwiched up together with a buttercream ganache,
all lined up in a row with Parisian panache!

There is a little substance, though (it's not just fluffy style):
for the knack of perfect baking takes, to learn, a little while.
It's the folding in of nuts and sugar to the eggs, when fate
is determined, based on what degree the egg whites will deflate.

Deflate *too* much and when they're baked, the shells will
    spread too wide,
and they'll lose that 'foot' upon which maca*rons* take so
    much pride.
If they don't deflate enough, they will have lumps and this
    will prove,
that neither shell nor baker is so suave, refined or smooth.

Macaroons, which have dried coconut, are rather more robust.
When it comes to looking *chic* they're, really, not so very fussed.
It's the coconut that's added to the sugar-egg-nuts base
that means a perfectly shaped mound will never be the
    likely case.

They are, instead, a puffy dome: more rugged-rough than neat.
The coconut brings moisture and it makes them very sweet.
They sometimes have some chocolate in a zig-zag, piped-out line
(or they're eaten simply as they are: no chocolate – plain – is fine).

As well as looking quite distinct upon their separate plates,
it is interesting to look at, too, just how the words translate.
Maccherone, in Italian, means 'fine paste that is ground';
it is there, again, in 'macaroni' – where the word is found.

Confusion comes when some take on the way the French
   will spell –
when the double 'o in macaroon gets dropped so we can't tell.
It's the same in other words – see how 'balloon' becomes *ballon*
which shows how *le macaroon* can then be said as 'mac-a-ron'.

A last note on the Gallic theme: it should, of course, be noted,
that none of this includes the man for whom the Frenchies voted.
Emmanuel Macron might well be chic and French and neat,
but he's not, *évidemment*, the petit fours you want to eat.

what's the difference between

baking powder

and

baking soda?

To all intents and purposes, these two look just the same:
finely ground white powder that has 'baking' in its name.
So, are they interchangeable – are either of them fine?
Or should we use the 'right' one, each and every baking time?

The one-word answer will be 'yes!' The right one must go in,
for they behave quite differently, once in the bowl or tin.
So let's look first at what they share; how these two
   powders merge,
before we look at what they don't share: how the two diverge.

'Raising agents' they both are, which for our baking matters,
in that they help to make air bubbles in our doughs, or batters.
When they're trapped, these bubbles grow, which makes the
   mixture rise,
and leavened, lightened batter is the baker's hoped-for prize.

Baking soda: first things first – let's get the name thing straight:
it's just the US name for sodium bicarbonate.
Bicarbonate of soda is the UK name so we
can call it what we want (or just $NaHCO_3$).

Either way, it is a pure compound, an alkali:
it needs an acid to react, which is, when baking, why
recipes that use bicarb must also, then, include
something that is acid (that can also work as food).

Buttermilk's a classic here, or yoghurt, soured cream,
vinegar or lemon juice – they all work like a dream.
When alkali and acid meet, they will react with speed
as soon as there's some moisture (which the process also needs).

It happens really quickly, CO_2 will get emitted:
it's *now* the cook and cake must really, fully get committed.
For if the mix is left to sit, that is the end of that –
the rise won't work and what gets baked will end up dense
    and flat.

Baking powder, by contrast, is slightly more docile.
It's not a pure compound, which means it can sit round a while.
For it's a mix that is combined with some tartaric acid,
which means that, paradoxically, it stays a bit more placid.

There also is a little starch in how the powder's made;
an anti-caking agent that helps things to get delayed.
In keeping everything else dry it buys a little time,
the mix can hang out in the bowl and it will still be fine.

For it reacts in stages: there is stage one and stage two.
The first when wet and then again, when heated it's all new.
The second batch of bubbling takes place when there is heat:
it's chemistry that we can thank for our light, fluffy treat.

Are the two interchangeable?

In terms of substitution, it can only work one way;
baking soda subbing in for powder's *not* okay.
For baking soda, on its own, has no acidity,
which won't have been accounted for within the recipe.

If it's baking soda that the recipe requires,
baking powder *can* be used (just check when it expires).
For as a mix it can be prone to pass beyond its peak,
which means it will not foam – it can't – as it's become too weak.

A little maths is needed, substitutes must always count
the baking powder quantity – it's triple the amount.
One teaspoon will end up as three but don't just add in haste;
times-ing it by three can change the cake's resulting taste.

For baking powder has the cream of tartar that can change
the balance of the acid, which can taste a little strange.
(Bicarb, as well, is quite distinct – its taste can overpower;
a soapy, tangy note can be there, even through plain flour.)

The point is that good recipes will factor all this in,
so it is really best to have the right one to begin.
For such a small amount, it is a cakey-crying shame,
for two helpful raising agents to get all the baker's blame.

what's the difference between

ice cream

and gelato?

Ice cream and gelato: aren't they pretty much the same?
With the latter just Italian: for ice cream, it's their name.
It turns out, though they're similar, these treats for summer days,
they are, in fact, distinct in quite a few, clear, separate ways.

The first is what they're made of and the ratio between
the milk that's there, and also eggs, and also how much cream.
For ice cream – as the name implies – has more cream,
    which means that
it has a richer mouthfeel, as it has a bit more fat.

Gelato, on the other hand, contains a bit more milk,
and eggs: they're few to none, which makes the base as light
    as silk.
With less eggs in the mix it means, for some, the great allure
will be gelato's flavour, being clear, pronounced and pure.

When it comes to fat, gelato has just 5 per cent.
Which means, for some, it's ice cream where their money's
    better spent.
Gelato, though, can teach us lots, from it we can all learn
the link between smooth texture and a slow and steady churn.

For the churning of the dairy, eggs and sugar, which are mixed,
will determine how much air gets in and how much it is 'fixed'.
With ice cream, it is the standard for the churn to be set fast,
which will whip in quite a lot of air (the cream then helps it last).

Gelato on the other hand, is churned more slowly, hence
there's less air in the mix so then the texture is more dense.
If ice cream, once it's made, can be half-filled with air
    whipped in,
then gelato's more like quarter air (the maths means 'half
    as thin').

The word that's used to show the volume growth is 'overrun'.
The higher that it is, the more the flavour tastes like none.
For though it's great for texture (if you like your ice cream light),
air will reduce the flavour, as it's not that big on bite.

Another way gelato's hit of flavour is more bold
is that, compared to ice cream, it is not stored *quite* as cold.
For ice cream's served from frozen: minus 18-ish degrees,
whilst gelato's served at minus-8: a much more gentle freeze.

The colder something is, the less its flavour will come through.
So, ice cream's often served in flavours novel, bold and new.
Gelato sticks to classics: roasted nuts, vanilla bean;
ice cream can be made to taste like gum in pink or green.

The thing we haven't mentioned yet (which makes all things
    a treat)
is the sugar that is added in to make things really sweet.
The quantities can vary, which will then affect the size
of the crystals, as the sugar stops how much they crystallize.

For when sugar goes in water it will gradually dissolve
and a syrup with a freezing point that's lower will evolve.
So the sweeter that a syrup is, the lower it will set,
but too much and a mush is what you will quite quickly get.

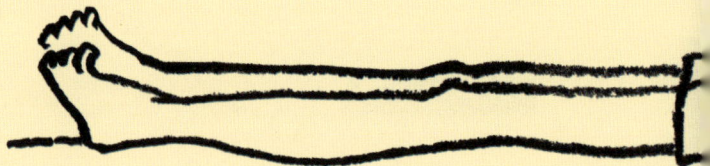

So it's sugar that affects the texture – try it out to prove:
less sugar makes it crunchy and more sugar makes it smooth.
It's the reason why granita (a related icy treat)
has more crunch than a sorbet scoop (another frozen sweet).

But regardless of the choice of ice or cup or cone or float –
whether eaten on a wooden bench or lying in a boat –
just be sure to take a moment to say 'thank you!' to the sun
for appearing and *demanding* that it's time for iced-cream fun.

For there's something quite delightful in the sunny,
    summer scene,
when the day is frozen still for some gelato or ice cream.

what's the difference between

bourbon

and

Scotch?

Those who aren't accustomed to a dram might tend to think
that Scotch and bourbon are – from whiskey – quite a
    separate drink.
But whiskey is the *category* of which there are then groups,
each quite unique and passing through their own,
    respective hoops.

Bourbon

'…but bourbon: is that not just whiskey from the USA?'
A lot of people think to be the case (and therefore say).
But no – although it's always made within the mighty States,
to be a bourbon (not a whiskey) there are certain traits.

Fifty-one per cent (or more) of corn there needs to be
within what's called the 'mash bill' (which is like the recipe).
The fact the major grain is corn, makes bourbon
    somewhat sweet,
(the other grains are malted barley, rye or maybe wheat).

Another rule that bourbon needs to always follow through
is being stored and aged in barrels that, each time, are new.
They can't have been in use before to age, for instance, wine;
they need to be, for bourbon, fresh and brand new every time.

For if the barrel's second-hand the wood might well be laced
with flavour (from some port, perhaps), which will then change
   the taste.
And flavours that are new cannot be brought in on the hoof:
the only thing allowed is water (which brings down the proof).

The years that bourbon needs to be in barrel-storage stage
can vary as there's no requirement for a certain age.
The age must just be stated if the years are less than four,
and 'straight' just means the age is two (at least: it can be more).

A common myth exists that bourbon's home must be Kentucky.
It's *not* a law, which, if you're making bourbon, is quite lucky.
A subset, though, of bourbon, does *indeed* have this decree:
Jack Daniel's, specifically, must come from Tennessee.

This whiskey that is popular throughout the USA
is made with maple charcoal: it's the 'Lincoln County way'.
The process can be used elsewhere: it is, for instance, seen
in making certain bourbons: it's the way for old Jim Beam.

So, bourbon can't be flavoured, coloured: doing so would tar
and take away from what the barrels bring with their oak char.
They bring a depth of colour and a round vanilla note,
for those who want consistency, then bourbon gets the vote.

Scotch

For others, it is Scotch they love: excited by the range
of flavours that can vary due to factors that will change.
The barrels, which the Scotch goes in, when waiting to mature
need not be new so – second-hand – the wood is not so 'pure'.

For if it's aged another drink, that flavour is still there,
which means that every batch of Scotch will be distinct and rare.
The time that Scotch spends ageing is three years (that is
    the least,
which often makes the end results a punchy-flavoured beast).

The mash bill (that's the recipe) for Scotch sees barley grain
make up the largest part: it's malted barley in the main.
With basic Scotch then other grains are blended: that's allowed.
A single malt, by contrast, shies away from any crowd.

It's malted barley only (and some water) in the bill,
and single malt stays put when it is time to be distilled.
While Scotches that are blended (Johnny Walker, raise
    your hand)
come from a range of places – all around the Scottish land.

They're blended, then, together: it's okay to mix and tweak.
The rules are loose so, flavour-wise, the profile is unique.
What makes a Scotch the drink whose fan base verges on
 the legions
is how distinct they are, depending on the Scottish regions.

The world of Scotch is vast, the flavour profile never ends;
From single malt to all the different places, ages, blends.
So that is Scotch and bourbon – just a wee nip; one wee dram –
for well-known whiskies come, as well, from Ireland and Japan.

All with their flavour profile based on oak and mash and age;
all barrelled, bottled up and drunk at quite a different stage.
The drink – whichever version – is a strong one, so it's power
is often best diluted in a drink like whisky sour.

Mint julep or old fashioned: two more drinks that clearly show
how easy it can be to drink a lot in just one go.
So whether it's a cocktail, on the rocks or simply neat:
bourbon, Scotch – all whiskey – should be handled as a treat.

Scottish blends: the Highlands
and Lowlands and Islands

The Scotch that comes from Isla has a taste not all acquire.
Its strongly peated notes are ones that conjure up a fire.
It's not for everyone: some find the flavour far too much –
preferring what the Highlands make – where peat is 'just
  a touch'.

Brands like Glenmorangie are a source of Highland pride.
For fruity, sweeter Scotches then head over to Speyside.
Macallan is a classic here, Glenlivet's also nice,
or head down to the Lowlands for a Scotch quite high on spice.

The Islands – close to water – tend to make Scotch that will be
quite salty – think of Talisker – produced so close to sea.
So that's a rapid run around of Scotland just to show
that when it comes to 'Scotch', there is no one way they all go.

what's the difference between

whisk*ey*

and

whisky?

When spoken they're identical, but written out we see
one version of the word which has an extra letter: 'e'.
The Scots can do without it: are they right or are they wrong?
Ireland and the States both *have* it: what is going on?

Early nineteenth century, and the world of distillation
got shaken by a man (called Coffey) causing consternation.
Whisky was, until this point, distilled in copper pots,
when Coffey pitched a process that sped up production lots.

He came up with a still shaped as a column, which would mean
continued distillation (with no need to pause and clean).
This meant that volume went up but the doubters didn't bite
(the doubters were the Irish: 'that guy, Coffey, he's not right.'

They spurned the new invention, sticking with the pot-
　　shaped still.
The thrifty Scots, meanwhile, dialled up production of
　　their 'swill'.
The market was receptive, sales soared right from the start.
The Irish were affronted, so they set themselves apart.

A way to show the difference of the two in quality
was bringing in the extra letter, hence we have the 'e'.
It was a form of marketing: a point of difference used
to make sure Scottish whisky and their 'whiskey'
　　weren't confused.

These days there are exceptions and the rules are not so stark.
The US takes the 'e' (apart from with their Maker's Mark).
In general, though, the countries that have 'e' within their name,
America and Ireland, for example, have the same.

They have the whiskey – with the 'e' – while countries
    that decline
the extra 'e' are also e-free (true *most* of the time).
Japan, for instance, Canada: the pattern's sort of there
(but whiskey–whisky: drink enough and, really: do we care?!…)

what's the difference between

a martini,

a Manhattan

and a margarita?

You're sitting at a fancy bar, you're propped up on a stool,
but the line of spirits makes you, frankly, feel quite the fool.
While those around you seem to know exactly what
   they're drinking,
'I haven't got a cocktail CLUE' is, really, what you're thinking.

If this is ringing bells, then raise your glass and raise your hand.
Listen in – here's everything you need to understand.

There are three general types of glass, distinct in size and shape.
Each one designed to suit the sort of drink it is to make.
There is the glass that has a stem, it's delicate and long –
the glass is coupe or V-shape, and the drink is often strong.
For what it lacks in volume (when it comes to size of cup)
is *more* than compensated for, in that it's served straight 'up'.

Serving 'up' means 'there's no ice': this drink will knock off socks.
For there is no dilution, as there is with 'on the rocks'.
'On the rocks' means cubes of ice (here 'rocks glasses' have
    their place:
being low and wide, which means, for ice, there will be space.)

Old fashioneds and negronis are two cocktails made this way.
They're easy to assemble at the end of any day.
A rocks glass at the ready, for the ice to all fit in,
with bourbon, for old fashioned; for negroni, it is gin.

Negroni is the bright, red one: it's stolen many hearts.
Campari, gin and red vermouth: all three in equal parts.
It opens up the appetite, it elevates the mood,
and primes the cocktail-drinker to anticipate some food.

Old fashioned (as the name suggests) is old-school, not too flash:
bourbon, sugar syrup and some bitters (just a dash).
On the rocks, a citrus twist, no need to overthink,
this needs no tools or fancy kit: it is a simple drink.

The highball is the taller glass (or 'Collins' is the name:
the latter's slightly taller but they're basically the same).
These glasses are the ones for drinks that need to fit lots in.
A classic being G&T (that's tonic, ice and gin).

A gin and tonic is a drink that cocktail-makers 'build'.
That's bar-speak for a cocktail where the glass is simply filled.
There is no need to stir it round or shake it up forever;
you simply put things in a glass and there they sit together.

The 'spritz' would be another drink 'built up' on top of ice.
Sparkling wine, Campari, soda (3:2:1 is nice).
Ratios are good to learn: the 4:2:1 is neat
(with four parts strong and two parts sour, then one part
    that is sweet).

This combo crops up frequently, within the cocktail hour.
It's at the heart of daiquiris, mojitos, whiskey sour.
Daiquiris are sugar syrup, lime juice and light rum;
shaken, strained – a cocktail glass – just add some Cuban fun.

Mojitos have the rum and lime and sugar syrup core,
but go into a tall glass so that there is room for more.
A lot of room, in fact, for ice and more than just a hint
of crisp, refreshing flavour from the muddled leaves of mint.

('Muddled' means to crush and press and, therefore,
    lightly bruise
the herbs or aromatics that a drink will need to use.)
Soda water's next and then mojito's good to go:
it's been dressed up but – 4:2:1 – you see the ratio.

Whiskey sour is another 4:2:1 big hitter.
It's got the bourbon, lemon, sugar (and a dash of bitter).
It's also got some egg white that, though helping bind,
    will mean,
this is, for some, a drink upon which they will not be keen.

Raw egg aside, this is a drink that really needs some shaking,
for it is made with things that need some help incorporating.
Things like citrus juice or milk or cream (they're all opaque)
when in a drink means that they need a great, big, massive shake.

If, instead, the drink's composed of things that are see-through,
then stirring well – not shaking – is the only thing to do.
So drinks such as Manhattan or martini should be stirred
(requests to have them shaken – sorry, Bond – are just absurd).

For as they have just spirits, then their aim is staying clear.
A drink is only shaken when things need help to cohere.
Think daiquiri and mai tai (which is rum and orange, lime):
These drinks – like margarita – need good shaking every time.

Shaking should be loud and long: it should be quite the riot.
Stirring should, by contrast, be methodical and quiet.
Both, however, need one thing to be considered nice
and that is lots and lots (and *lots*) of chilled big cubes of ice.

Some final points: it's rarely wise to drink hard without lunch
(unless it's bloody Mary, which goes very well with brunch).
Gimlets are the little strong ones made with lime and gin,
and margaritas are the ones with salt around their rim.

A basil smash or bramble are gin sours, though their name
reflects the herb or fruit addition, or, if it's champagne,
then this is in a champagne flute: its name French 75 –
one to choose (like espresso martini) for a *very* quick revive.

Moscow mules have ginger beer, Manhattan's have the cherry.
A paper parasol will always make a drink look merry.
White Russians have the vodka, coffee liqueur, ice and milk
(eggnog is also part of that rich, sweet and creamy ilk).

Whatever drink you choose, enjoy, but think to stop at one.
Though cocktails can make out that all they are is liquid fun,
they can be strong (and guarantee you *will* look like a fool
when, after drinking three or four you do fall off that stool).

what's the difference between

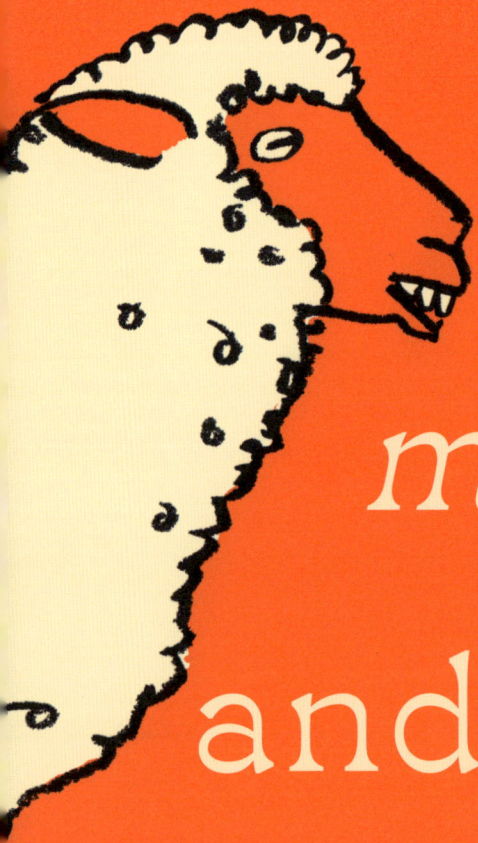

mutton

and *lamb*

and *pork*

and *ham?*

Let's start off with the basics, it's a useful place to start;
before we zoom right in and start to cook a certain part,
we must make sure we know what's what so that we can
    then talk
with confidence, when choosing cuts of lamb and beef
    and pork.

Lamb is what a sheep is called until the sheep turns one.
Mutton's then the name for when the sheep is not so young.
With age comes muscle, also fat, so mutton's more robust,
slow cooking for this tougher meat is very much a must.

Ewes are adult female sheep, they make both wool and lamb,
while adult male sheep can be a wether or a ram.
Wethers are just used for wool – they're not the sheep
    for breeding;
for reproduction, rams are what a farmer will be needing.

Beef's the name of cattle meat when baby calves get older.
The meat is darker – red, not pink – the flavour's also bolder.
The older that the cattle are, the more they're exercised;
for those who like a tender cut, then veal will be most prized.

A heifer is a bovine that has not yet given birth,
she needs to have a calf to show her use and breeding worth.
Once she's had a calf she's then a cow and must stick near
a sire (or bull) who breeds (unlike a snipped, less-useful steer).

Pork is any cut of meat that's bought raw from the shops.
It can be shoulder, belly, leg or loin, or cheek or chops.
It's only from the pig's hind legs that ham is found and taken
(so, head towards the back or belly those who want their bacon).

Ham and gammon are the same but gammon is sold raw.
Ham is what it's called once cooked, so gammon comes before.
Gammon's cured (salt, brine or smoke): once cooked it's
   then a ham.
All *not* to be confused with processed canned pork –
   that is SPAM.

So that's a really quick whiz through the basic livestock stages
to show how names will vary as things move through all
   their ages.
The more mature the meat, the more intense it will become,
with younger meat more tender (as a general rule of thumb).

what's the difference between

a *Pepsi*

and

a Coke?

Pepsi's slightly sweeter, also lemony and tart,
thanks to the citric acid that is in there from the start.
Coke's a bit more mellow and vanilla notes are found,
its taste is slightly smoother, less acidic, some say 'round'.

That's the quick-fire answer to what separates these cans.
So why do they elicit *such* strong feelings in their fans?
The answer needs to take a longer view to understand,
that it's not about the taste, so much, as it's about the 'brand'.

A brief history, from station to nation

Coca-Cola was the drink to hit the market first.
In 1886, the syrup quenched Atlanta's thirst.
A chemist – Doctor Pemberton – found that his local shop
did very well when selling his brown syrup as a pop.

The drink scaled really quickly: Coca-Cola was the name
(reflecting its inclusion of both caffeine and cocaine).
People loved the taste, it cleared the head and gave a boost –
there were some copycats but Coca-Cola ruled the roost.

Until another pharmacist, in 1893,
invented a new cola that could claim to be drug-free.
His name was Caleb Bradham, so he gave the drink his name
(though 'Brad's drink' was soon seen by most, in terms of
    branding, lame).

It changed its name to Pepsi-Cola, giving the suggestion,
that drinking it could help relieve the pain of indigestion.
Indigestion is 'dyspepsia' (its proper name),
so the shortened form of 'Pepsi' makes good sense –
    it sounds the same.

The century turned, these drinks sold well, to help relieve
   the tummy.
Sales grew well from year to year, so folks were making money.
Pepsi was the first to scale beyond the soda station,
taking up the 'bottle tech', it spread out to the nation.

Coca-Cola was, by contrast, not sold by the bottle,
so Pepsi hit the market: they had foot down at full throttle.
Things for Pepsi were, at this stage, going really well,
until the twenties when the price of sugar rose, then fell.

Pepsi's sugar stockpiles turned, then, overnight to dust,
a disaster for the business, seeing Pepsi soon go bust.
The door was open wide for just one soda, sweet and brown:
it was Coca-Cola, for some years, that wore the soda crown.

Pepsi, though, returned; a little sweeter was thought nice,
they cut their cost to play hard ball with Coke, in terms of price.
The market quickly switched as people proved to be
   quite fickle,
falling for the slogan 'Twice as much for just a nickel'.

But for all that Pepsi's marketing saw Pepsi's sales soar,
it was Coca-Cola that became the go-to drink of war.
It resulted from a tax loop Coca-Cola got around,
which enabled it to be the drink for troops upon the ground.

It was here that Coca-Cola sealed its place for those who think
that it's Coke which is the one – the nation's choice: the
   favourite drink.
Coke was riding high and "teaching all the world to sing",
claiming that, with Coke in hand, you cannot "beat the real thing".

The 'Pepsi challenge'

Pepsi kept on marketing; it's fan base was diverse
then 'the Pepsi Challenge' came along: for Coke this was a curse.
For the challenge set the two drinks up and, in a blindfold test,
people said which one they liked the most and this, was then,
   the 'best'.

Now when people have just one sip, they will very often choose,
the sweeter one so, in this test, Coke was the one to lose.
Even if, when drinking more, a Coke would be preferred,
this was not a fact well known or heeded or, indeed, much heard.

Coke's response was fully wrong and quickly judged a waste,
when changing its ingredients to match with Pepsi's taste.
The whole, entire plan was both misguided and misjudged,
for the loyal Coca-Cola fans would not be swayed or budged.

They'd grown up hearing 'Coke is it' so now what should they do,
with a different Coke that they were told was better: it was 'new'?
Quickly seeing all the damage done, the sales hit and hurt,
Coca-Cola, to their credit, did a very quick revert.

Pepsi kept up marketing, endorsed throughout the years,
by a range of big-name stars like Cindy Crawford, Britney Spears.
Beyoncé, David Beckham, they all helped the sales to lift,
(Coca-Cola saved all pennies up to work with Taylor Swift).

They each came up with slogans in an effort to become
the soda that is thought to be for each and everyone.
But although they pitch themselves as drinks that are for
   all – unite! –
when it comes to market share, they've been forever in a fight.

A sweet thought, to end on

There is now space and appetite for both upon the shelf,
but it all feels like a long way from those first claims to
   good health.
When thirsty next and weighing up the pros of all the cans,
it might be worth just checking out the sugar there in grams.

The quantity is so vast that a whole new industry
has arisen where a fizzy drink is sold as sugar-free.
Be wary, though, of words and spellings that can't
   be pronounced,
when a claim to healthy living is asserted or announced.

For whether Pepsi Max or Zero is the 'healthy' name,
the way that they are sugar-free is using aspartame.
They're free of carbs (or very low); few calories (or none),
but those who want a 'healthy' drink... it's WATER, everyone!

what's the difference between

red can,

blue can,

silver can

and

black *can?*

(Aka: an insight into the psychological difference between men and women when it comes to colour)

Coca-Cola is the red can – timeless: old or new.
Pepsi changed its logo but the can is always blue.
Pepsi Max is black; it's silver for a Diet Coke.
These diet-soda drinkers are a colour-coded folk.

For research shows that silver cans, for half the market, fail.
They resonate with women but do not work for the male.
Put it in a black can, though, and slap the word on 'zero'
and men will choose their diet drink, still feeling like a hero.

For some, it's always 'soda', while for others it is 'pop'.
It depends where, in the States, you are: where is the
  chosen shop.
'Soda' is the term preferred along the North-East coast,
in places like St Louis, it's the word that's used the most.

In Oregon and Kansas, though (the Midwest and the West),
it's 'pop' that is the chosen word; the one that sounds the best.
The lid comes off and 'pop!': that's CO_2 on its escape.
The word describes the popping sound the drink is known
  to make.

'Soda' comes from sodium, found in a natural spring.
It comes from carbonation, when the term became a thing.
Soda is the word used most by fizzy drink-ing folk,
though in the Southern States, all soft drinks are just called
  'a coke'.

'A coke' is what is asked for but 'a coke' might not be right:
the person serving needs to ask, 'Is that a Coke or Sprite?
Or is it Doctor Pepper, Fanta or a 7up?
Which carbonated drink would you like in your can or cup?

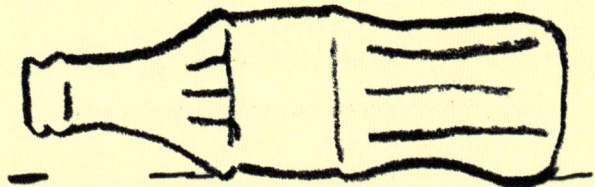

what's the difference between

Parmesan

and

pecorino?

You'll often see them interchanged within a recipe:
these hard and salty cheeses, which both come from Italy.
They are, in fact, quite different, so conflation will be wrong,
for starters, it's two animals from whose milk they are from.

For Parmesan, the milk is from a cow (the milk's kept raw),
the cow eats only grasses; nothing less and nothing more.
Fresh and also fruity – also nutty – is the taste
and Parmesan is slowly aged: there is no speed or haste.

At least a year – or up to three – and this is how and why
the texture's slightly grainy: crystalline and also dry.
The longer that it's left to age, the drier it will be.
These rules must be obeyed to get the status 'DOP'.

In order to gain status, some requirements are a must:
shape and fat percentage, storage; shape and age and crust.
The region is important, too: there are in fact just four
where Parmesan is made, according to the strict cheese law.

'Parmigiano' is, in fact, the word you want to find
written on the label or imprinted on the rind.
The presence of the name marks out the cheese's pedigree
while 'Parmesan' alone does not quite have the guarantee.

Parmesan is 'fine' – it's just not, of its kind, the best.
It hasn't always been produced in Italy's north-west.
It might be slightly younger – here a taste test helps to prove:
the flavour will be less intense, the texture slightly smooth.

Moving on to pecorino: this one's made by sheep.
The palate needs to pivot, or just make a little tweak.
The cheese is aged for less time, so the younger taste is brighter,
the colour of the milk means that the cheese is also whiter.

The word for sheep's *pecora*, it is tangy in the mouth,
it's made in central Italy and also in the South.
It's high in fat and salt content and has a brown-black rind
In cacio e pepe, it's the cheese you'll always find.

It's used in carbonara, too, which needs a cheese this strong
to boost this classic Roman dish and carry it along.
Parmesan is better suited on a Bolognese
(or simply eaten as it is when there's a need to graze).

Of course, when no one's looking, you can do just as you please,
and grate, on top of pasta, any sort of dry, hard cheese.
But know that any nonna will not hide her furrowed brow
if presented with a sheepy cheese when it should be from cow.

Acknowledgements

For all the big questions in life, how the cookie crumbles might not be top of everybody's mind. The fact that I've been able to get a collection of rhymes about the matter out into this busy world is, therefore, rather remarkable. That I have is thanks to a rather special crew.

At Pavilion, thank you to my editor Lucy Smith, for working so hard to get me there with the rhymes, the title, the whole shebang. I'm so sorry I still don't know the difference between 'that' and 'which'. I'm going to stop pretending that I'll ever get it. Thank you to Daisy Gudmunsen, the super talented Alice Kennedy-Owen and everyone at Pavilion/ Harper Collins for everything you do to design, champion and sell books. Enormous thanks to Alec Doherty: once again you've exceeded my hopes and dreams with your delightful, cheeky and brilliant illustrations. You're the best! Thank you to Charlie Brotherstone, my agent, and to Gilly Smith, for the initial introduction and endless support.

Thanks so much to team Ottolenghi, particularly Yotam, Helen and Verena, with whom I've worked most closely with, on *Comfort*, whilst also writing this book. You're all totally brilliant and have been so supportive and encouraging throughout. Thank you. And Helen, honoured to share a publication date with you!

Thanks to Felicity Cloake, Niki Segnit, J. Kenji Lopez-Alt (and all at the Serious Eats website), Alan Davidson, Harold McGee, Samin Nosrat, Nigella Lawson, the Guardian website, Christopher Kimball and Francis Lamb. As with *How to Butter Toast*, you've been the first I've turned to and read and listened to in the course of researching my rhymes. Particularly HUGE thanks to Felicity Cloake for writing me the most delightful of all forewords. Thank you for being such a 'yes' person, especially as you always have so much on. You bring so much unadorned joy into the food world that your views on tahini are (partially) forgiven. Big thanks to Harriet Fitch-Little, at the FT magazine, for commissioning me to write the rhyming 'cut-lets' for your epic feature on meat, and for the pork and ham, mutton or lamb rhyme that resulted.

To my friends, as ever: old friends, like bookends, keeping me together, secure and smiling. To Nessa and Katie – Friday lunch club joy! – and to Neache – my tupperware sister. Annie and Sonia: here's to small fires, big spirits and taking up space. To Julia – such a pal – and to Winnie and Ellie, Jessie and Katherine: thank you for always being there and, to Jess and Katherine, for inspiring me to get my running shoes back on. To Carenza and Mary, Lucy and Bea, Sarah and Ellie – may all our paths be strewn with the leaves of little gems – with special enormous thanks to Ellie Walford. Thank you for once again reading my rhymes. You manged to both tighten them at the same time as making me feel like they totally cut the mustard. Keep singing, my friend. Here's to being brave.

Thanks to Mum and Dad, as ever, for enthusing and engaging and for kick starting this whole rhyming prose lark in the first place. And to my crew: Chris and Scarlett, Theo and Casper. So many high fives, so much support, so much acceptance of all the aubergines. You guys *are* the dream team.

Finally, thanks to Gary at Moen's the bookseller-butchers, in Clapham. Your support for my first book makes me smile every time I cycle past. You're all set to paint the shop front a nice, bright orange for this one, right?